A Guide to
SHETLAND'S
BREEDING
B I R D S

Bobby Tulloch

The Shetland Times Ltd
Lerwick
1992

First published by The Shetland Times Ltd, 1992

© Bobby Tulloch, 1992

The photographs on pages 30, 34, 50 (bottom picture),
52, 64 (top picture), 65, 69, 75, 76, 78 and 79 are by Andy Gear.
The photographs on pages 38, 39 and 70 are by Wendy Dickson.
The photograph on page 47 (top picture) is by Libby Weir-Breen.
All other photographs are by the author, © Bobby Tulloch, 1992.

All rights reserved. No part of this publication may be reproduced,
stored in a retrieval system, or transmitted, in any form, or by any
means, electronic, mechanical, photocopying, recording or otherwise,
without the prior permission of the publishers.

ISBN 0 900662 81 6

British Library Cataloguing-in-Publication Data

A catalogue record for this book is
available from the British Library

Designed in Shetland by
The Stafford Partnership

Printed and published by
The Shetland Times Ltd,
Prince Alfred Street, Lerwick, Shetland, Scotland.

INTRODUCTION

It is now over twenty years since the late Fred Hunter and I wrote the first 'Guide to Shetland Birds'. This ran to three editions and several reprints, but has been out of print for several years.

So it seemed opportune to take a fresh look at our birdlife, and to summarise the present situation, while keeping in view the past history.

It had been pointed out that many people, locals and visitors alike, have only a passing interest in birds, and that some guidance on basic points of identification, even of the common species, would help stimulate interest. Few people — especially first-time visitors to Shetland — who have looked over the cliffs at places like Hermaness or Noss and marvelled at the great 'sea-bird cities' can fail to be impressed and to wonder just what kinds of birds they are looking at.

No small book can ever be 'all things to all men' and compromises have to be made; it was obvious that to try to cover every aspect of Shetland bird life was not only beyond my capabilities, but would make a book expensive to produce, and too cumbersome to be the 'pocket' size guide which we felt was needed.

It was decided to limit this 'Guide' to looking at the breeding birds only, but to include as many colour pictures as possible, and to offer some guidance on how to identify the commoner breeding species by giving such details of plumage, calls and habits as we have found useful.

A personal interest is the origins of the Shetland dialect names for many of our common birds; some of these such as 'Bonxie' and 'Tystie' are now used widely in Britain and beyond. Evidence that many of these names originate in our former close affinities with the Norse language are suggested, and I have included some of the Icelandic, Faroese and Norwegian names — many of which support this view — in the hope that the reader will also find this of interest.

Much is talked today of the increasing threats to the wellbeing and even the existence of much of our wildlife.

Many of the problems stem from the demands of an ever growing human population; the pollution of air and sea from chemical and waste discharges, the over-exploitation of the world's resources — from the destruction of rainforests to overfishing of the seas.

While acknowledging the serious threats posed by these and many other factors, I think we have to recognise the amazing adaptive powers of nature, the evolutionary processes which allows species to cope with adversity — and even at times to turn them to advantages.

I hope the day never dawns when the tirricks fail to arrive back on time from their world travels, to delight us with their presence and to confirm that, in spite of much gloom and doom there is still much joy to be found in the natural world.

Bobby Tulloch
November, 1991.

CONTENTS

Hermaness National Nature Reserve.

WHERE TO LOOK FOR BIRDS

There are over a hundred islands in the Shetland group and it is not possible to describe each and every one of them in detail.

I have selected some areas and islands I happen to know reasonably well, but there are many others worthy of a visit. There are inhabited islands like Bressay, Papa Stour, Burra Isle, Trondra and Muckle Roe. All have substantial bird populations. Muckle Roe for instance, while it is connected by a bridge, is an island and has one of the largest Cormorant populations in Shetland.

Papa Stour has the distinction of holding the largest Arctic Tern colony in Shetland.

Noss

There are of course dozens of small uninhabited islands, some of them superb natural bird reserves. The island of Hascosay for instance, off the east side of Yell, probably has more breeding Dunlin per acre than anywhere I know. The little isles west of Scalloway hold large numbers of breeding Storm Petrels and Grüney near Fethaland even has Leach's Petrels.

And so it goes . . .

A brief look at some selected areas and islands.

Ringed Plover

Spiggie RSPB Reserve

The Mainland is the largest island of the Shetland group and features a wide variety of scenery and interesting bird-watching areas.

Taking Lerwick as a base point, road distances are approximately 42 miles to North Roe, 25 and 32 miles respectively to Walls and Sandness, and 26 miles south to Sumburgh Head. Roads are excellent, thanks to an extensive roadwork programme in recent years, and even long winding roads to remote townships are tarred throughout.

The visitor may therefore be recommended with confidence to bring a car or hire one on arrival, especially since the network of car-ferries allows easy access to most of the main inhabited islands as well.

Most of Shetland's breeding birds can be found at one place or another on Mainland and the rugged rock-strewn north and west parts of the island present a real challenge to the energetic visitor.

The challenge if accepted may bring a handsome reward, for many of the remote areas are seldom visited and the keen walker could, for instance, find Peregrines on a remote cliff, Whimbrels on the hills or Common Scoters on distant lochs.

NORTH MAINLAND — This, the most rugged part of the main island also includes some of Shetland's finest scenery, from the view from the top of Ronas Hill (our highest at 1475 feet) to the magnificent cliffscapes at Eshaness.

North of Ronas Hill is a wilderness of lochs and moorland with high cliffs to the west where a person can walk all day without meeting another soul. Divers, skuas, Dunlin and Merlin are among the breeding birds and Snowy Owls are occasionally seen on the boulder-strewn slopes of Ronas Hill. Here the feeling that you are on the Arctic tundra can be enhanced by finding plants like Alpine Lady's-mantle or Trailing Azalea — and you might even hear a singing Snow Bunting!

Ramna Stacks RSPB Reserve

A walk out to the headland of Fethaland — dominated by a new lighthouse, will bring the visitor as near as one is likely to get to the RSPB reserve of Ramna Stacks. Lying offshore in fierce tidal currents the stacks are rarely accessible, but hold colonies numbering thousands of seabirds including

Ronas Hill

Guillemots, Razorbills, Puffins and Kittiwakes.

At Fethaland too can be seen the ruins of the fishermen's cottages or booths, a reminder of the days when Shetland fishermen faced the rigours and dangers of the open ocean, fishing for their living from open six-oared boats.

The road past Hillswick leads to Eshaness, where on each side of the lighthouse stretches the longest unbroken range of cliffs in Shetland. At intervals there are jagged rents into the land where seabirds whirl in the chasms which plunge straight down into the sea. Fulmars occupy many of the ledges, and on the stacks — towering grass topped columns which were once joined to the main cliff — Herring and Great Black-backed Gulls nest secure from human interference.

Cliffs at Hillswick

Near the township of Stennes the coast is less rugged and Puffins can be seen along the low cliffs, while to seaward the islet called Dore Holm also has colonies of seabirds, their voices carrying distinctly over the sea to the shore. In summer Kittiwakes from Dore Holm fly in an endless stream to a little loch behind the crofts of Stennes, there to bathe or, earlier in the season gather beaksfull of moss from the loch edges with which to build their nests on the holm.

Bonxies too use the loch for bathing, and they also patrol the Kittiwake cliffs, snatching the unwary bird or nestling for a meal. Arctic Skuas also nest in many places on the hills, and they too get their food by piracy, chasing terns, auks and Kittiwakes until they drop their catch.

Red-throated Divers nest on many of the lochs of the North Mainland, even on those close to the roadsides where they can be watched from a car. And this is the safest way to watch divers, as disturbance — which is illegal — so often leaves the nest or young vulnerable to predation by skuas or gulls.

The road to the North Mainland is via Mavis Grind — which means 'the gateway on the narrow isthmus' in the old language — and here the Atlantic Ocean is separated by a stones-throw from Sullom Voe, which is an arm of Yell Sound opening out into the North Sea. It is from here that the visitor will become aware of the scale of the oil developments. Mavis Grind itself has been' radically changed by quarrying operations — and more are planned in the area — while further along Sullom Voe to the east, the oil storage tanks, loading jetties, power station and all the other facilities of the oil port have all but obliterated the headland of Calback Ness.

But Sullom Voe still has its birdlife; divers, Mergansers, and Eider Ducks feed in the voe and Otters are frequently seen — even within the oil-terminal itself.

WEST MAINLAND — A glance at a map will show that the West Mainland is liberally studded with freshwater lochs, large and small, many of which are rarely approached other than by shepherds or a determined angler. Common Scoters nest in this area but to what extent is not accurately known. The best time to look for them is during May and June when the drakes are displaying on the lochs. The females are very elusive when they have eggs or young.

Red-throated Divers are widespread, Tufted Ducks nest in a few places and many of the larger lochs have grassy islets supporting noisy colonies of Black-headed Gulls. The surrounding moorland has its fair share of breeding birds such as Curlew, Lapwing, Golden Plover and Wheatear, and it is no rare thing to see a Merlin dash past in pursuit of some hapless Meadow Pipit or Skylark.

Golden Plover

7

Near West Burrafirth

One of the interesting parts of the West Mainland is the Weisdale Valley, some 14 miles from Lerwick. Kergord farm occupies a major part of this fertile valley and boasts a rare thing in Shetland — plantations of trees!

It was established around the turn of the century in several groups covering eight or nine acres. There are stands of conifers on the hillside and some mixed deciduous plantations near the farmhouse. The trees have attracted a number of bird species which might not otherwise be part of the Shetland fauna; a colony of Rooks became established in 1952, and there are small numbers of Wood Pigeons and occasional Jackdaws.

More sporadic breeding records have included Fieldfare, Redwing, Goldcrest, Willow Warbler, Blackcap, Tree Sparrow and Chaffinch. Red Grouse nest in the surrounding hills and nearby Sand Water has a good area of Bulrush and breeding records of Little Grebe, Coot, Moorhen and Wigeon.

SOUTH MAINLAND — The south part of the mainland is not so rugged as the north and west; there are large cultivated areas and the terrain is gentler in aspect although with fine bold headlands and cliff in the south.

Shetland's main airport is at Sumburgh and is almost at the centre of some very good birding spots. One runway lies parallel to the sandy tidal basin of the Pool of Virkie, beloved by migrant waders and where many Shetland rarities have turned up.

It is also the headquarters for the bulk of the small Shetland population of Shelduck.

Just beyond the airport Sumburgh Head rears up, surmounted by a lighthouse and with road access. Here, within yards of the parking place, you can enjoy the sights and sounds of a large seabird colony. Guillemots and Razorbills on the ledges, Puffins peering out of their nesting burrows or arriving with beaks full of small fish, and usually a few Twite will be seen here, flying around with their lovely 'twangy' call.

Sumburgh Head

On a clear day the view is magnificent, the hills of Fair Isle 25 miles south across the restless 'roost' and twenty-odd miles to the north the silhouette of Noss — another super seabird colony. A few miles west of Sumburgh Head is another bold headland, Fitful Head, which is 900 feet high. Here Peregrine Falcons had their eyrie and many years ago the great White-tailed Sea Eagles used to nest.

Spiggie Loch RSPB Reserve

Below the slopes of Fitful Head and to the north lie the large lochs of Spiggie and Brow. An RSPB reserve, but more of importance for its wintering herds of Whooper Swans. Still, it is worth stopping at vantage points on the road near the lochs because Long-tailed Ducks often stay on into June though not — so far as we know — to nest, but you never know!

The small Loch of Hillwell in Quendale is enriched from the surrounding farmland and in its reedy margins broods of Pintail or Shoveler have been seen. Yellow wagtails have nested here and Coot are fairly regular. In spring and early summer the Sumburgh area is especially good for migrants — so expect the unexpected!

EAST AND CENTRAL MAINLAND — Lacking areas of high sea cliffs and being rather 'landlocked' by the outer isles, no remarkable colonies of seabirds are to be found here, but all the usual shore birds, and many Fulmar and Black Guillemot breed.

Hill birds such as Red Grouse, Curlew, Merlins, Hooded Crows and the small birds like Wheatear, Meadow Pipit and Skylark abound. The coastline around North and South Nesting is especially good for that elusive mammal the Otter, and the higher hills offer a good chance of seeing Blue Hare.

YELL — Take the road north from Lerwick, past Girlsta (home to the only known colony of Arctic Char in Shetland) past the attractive township of Voe and the 'mini-fjord' of Dales Voe to the car-ferry terminus of Toft (a good place to watch for Otters as you await the ferry). From here a fifteen minute crossing past the now uninhabited islands of Bigga and Samphrey takes you to the second largest island in Shetland, Yell.

Yell has rarely excited the prose of the writers of travel brochures. The first impression is of a rather sombre island of rounded peat-covered hills.

It is rectangular in shape except where it is almost cut in half by two encroaching arms of the sea; Whale Firth from the west and Mid Yell Voe from the east.

But do not be misled by impressions from a bus or car window; the road runs from the ferry terminus at Ulsta through perhaps the most desolate part of the island to connect with yet another car-ferry at Gutcher. This provides access to the outer islands of Unst and Fetlar.

For anyone who likes to wander over heather hills, out of sight and sound of civilization, and with only the birds and a few sheep for company, Yell is an ideal place.

To sit and rest by the side of a tumbling hill burn, soothed by the songs of Skylark, Golden Plover and Curlew, uplifted by the wild wailing of Red-

9

throated Divers or inspired by the delicate beauty of a Sundew, can be just as satisfying to the spirit as the towering cliffs with their myriads of seabirds.

Not that you cannot find such places in Yell. Go to the Horse of Burravoe and watch Kittiwake, Guillemot, Razorbill and Puffin: spend a night in the eerie lee of a ruined Pictish broch and watch for the fluttering shapes of Storm Petrels.

There are splendid cliff walks such as north from the Daal of Lumbister (another RSPB reserve) or along the West Neaps of Graveland where the spire of the Erne Stack is a reminder that here the very last pair of White-tailed Eagles had their eyrie.

For its size Yell probably has the greatest density of Red-throated Divers anywhere in the country, nesting by the sides of lochs and pools which are sometimes so small that the birds cannot get airborne unless a breeze is blowing.

Red-throated Diver

All the moorland birds have summer homes in Yell and the low shores of the east coast are home to many Otters.

Watch out for Common Scoter on the lochs, in particular the Loch of Littlester at Burravoe.

And while in that area, why not call along the Old Haa local history museum for a 'cuppa' and a browse — especially through the natural history room.

Diver lochan on Lumbister (Yell)

Hermaness National Nature Reserve

UNST — From Gutcher in Yell, the car-ferry takes only 10 minutes to cross Bluemull Sound to Unst, but the contrast between the two islands is quite marked. In place of the rolling peat hills and boggy valleys of Yell, Unst has rocky ridges, tundra-like slopes covered in thin turf with stony outcrops and screes. There are large areas of fertile grazing and farmland in the valleys. Only in the north and west are there some peat covered hills like those on Yell. All this is because of the more varied geological structure, much of the island being of permeable serpentine.

Because of this variety of habitat, Unst attracts a greater variety of breeding birds than anywhere else of comparable size in Shetland. The inland areas are particularly attractive to waders, and all those on the Shetland breeding list can be found, many of them widespread and common.

None is more evocative of northern latitudes than the Whimbrel, whose breeding range scarcely extends further south than Shetland. They breed sparingly over the serpentine areas and their liquid, trilling call is one of the delightful 'songs of the north'.

But for sheer bird spectacle, Hermaness must take pride of place. This bold headland, the furthest north in Britain, is in summer surely one of the greatest 'bird-cities' in the country.

For several miles the cliffs are up to 600 feet in height and are thronged with a variety of seabirds. Tens of thousands of Puffins nest in the screes and grassy slopes, the lower ledges are jam-packed with Guillemots and the boulder tangles below the cliffs are alive with Razorbills and Shags. Many of the sheer cliff-faces are plastered with Kittiwake nests and Fulmars glide and wheel ceaselessly in the up-drafts and air currents.

But most spectacular of all are the Gannets. In 1917 a few pairs nested on the Vesta Skerry, out near where the Muckle Flugga lighthouse keeps its lonely vigil. They increased and spread to other stacks and to the cliffs of Hermaness itself until today they number over 8000 pairs.

From the cliff-top they can be watched as they come and go with food for the young, and exciting aerial battles can often be seen as they are harried by Bonxies from the large colony on the headland above the cliffs.

Great Skua

In 1972 a Black-browed Albatross was found to have joined the Gannets at the Point of Saito. This lost wanderer from the southern oceans returned each year to the same spot — and even built a large nest! But after 20 years of waiting it seems to be losing hope of finding a mate, and this year (1991) it only appeared briefly early in the season.

Hermaness is a National Nature Reserve and while there are no access restrictions, this happy state can only be maintained if we all treat this important area with the respect it deserves.

The east and south coasts of Unst are gentler in aspect with some fine sandy beaches which may even tempt the brave to find out just how invigorating the sea temperature of Shetland is!

Snowy Owl

FETLAR — The same car-ferry which shuttles between Yell and Unst also makes a few daily trips to Fetlar, a fine fertile island which shares the same geological characteristics of Unst, and offers a very similar variety of birdlife.

The same kinds of seabirds can be seen — although in smaller numbers — on many of the cliffs and headlands. Fetlar lacks Gannets but makes up for it by offering a better chance of seeing Manx Shearwaters and Storm Petrels.

There are no large colonies of shearwaters, but small flocks can often be seen in Tresta bay in the evenings, waiting for darkness to fall before venturing in to change places with their mate deep in a crevice of the grassy cliff-slopes.

A night spent sitting out in places like Grüney Geo on the west side of Fetlar, can be an interesting experience.

As the evening fades into the half-light that we call the 'simmer dim', bat-like shapes begin to flutter past, and you can hear an occasional purring sound coming from small holes in the turf. These are the Storm Petrels returning from the sea to take their stint at incubating the tiny white eggs.

The silence of the night may be broken only by the swish of the sea or perhaps an occasional brief argument by a pair of Fulmar, when suddenly the peace is broken by a demoniac cackling and a rushing of wings as a dark shape thumps to the ground and scuttles down a burrow — the Manx Shearwaters have decided the time is right for the change-over!

By the time the light has strengthened enough for you to see details of the cliffs, all will be quiet again until the 'day-shift' of other seabirds stir into action.

It was in Fetlar that one of the ornithological events of the century took place in 1967, when a pair of Snowy Owls decided to nest on the rocky hill of Stakkaberg. They continued to breed for nine years and led to the establishment of the RSPB Fetlar Reserve where, although the owls no longer breed, still has a resident summer warden who is available to offer help and guidance to visitors, or even to advise if there is a 'watchable' Snowy Owl on the island.

As in Unst there is a scattered population of Whimbrel nesting on the hills of Fetlar, and a few pairs of the delightful little Red-necked Phalarope

RSPB Fetlar Reserve

which breed secretively in marshy spots such as the Mires of Funzie (pronounced 'Finnie'). Here the RSPB has constructed an observation hide overlooking the marsh and an hour or so spent with binoculars or telescope is rarely wasted.

The nearby Loch of Funzie is a good place to watch phalarope because they often feed there, and the best way is to sit quietly in your car (or by the roadside) and before long you will hear a gentle 'chirrick' and a Red-necked Phalarope may fly in and plop into the water a few feet away, proceeding to feed, ignoring your presence — at least that's what has happened to me on many occasions!

Red-necked Phalarope

A point I would like to make is that while Shetland people are renowned for their hospitality, they cannot be blamed for objecting to having their walls and fences damaged and crops trampled — no matter how rare and exciting a bird may be!

In Shetland few crops — even of grass — are raised without a lot of hard and often frustrating work. A polite request will usually get the required permission to walk across croft land and — often enough — information about local birds which the visitor may never have found out for themselves.

OUT SKERRIES AND WHALSAY — These two islands are on the east side of Shetland, and without doubt their best claim to ornithological interest lies in their attraction to migrant birds in spring and autumn.

Both are connected by car-ferries and are well worth a visit. The Whalsay ferry goes from Laxo and the Skerries connection is from Lerwick or Vidlin. (Timetables are obtainable from the Shetland Tourist Office in Lerwick).

Whalsay has a large and important fishing fleet and so has a comparatively high human population. But there are still some fine walks where many birds will be seen. There are small numbers of breeding Whimbrel and other moorland species.

Lack of extensive cliffs limits the seabird population but there are Tysties and Fulmars and some Kittiwake, as well as all the usual shore-birds.

There is often a late passage of migrants through Shetland — 'June rarities' is an almost regular feature — and a day spent in Whalsay or in Skerries in late May or early June could well pay dividends.

Out Skerries lies even further east, and so must be the first landfall for many migrant birds pushed off their traditional routes across the North Sea by south-easterly gales.

It should come as no surprise to learn that the list of birds recorded in Out Skerries reads like the life-list of a top 'twitcher'!

The islands are small, having a total area of only some 600 acres, and are grouped round a superb natural harbour.

This provides an ideal base for a small fleet of fishing boats, which is why Skerries, as it is locally known, has a population of nearly a hundred people.

Apart from passing migrants, Skerries has a good population of sea and shore birds, including some large tern colonies, lots of Tysties, Oystercatchers, Ringed Plovers and various gulls.

There used to be a small colony of House Sparrows nesting in a cliff-face, but they recently have become more urbanised!

There is no peat on Skerries and the resultant broken rocky landscape is very attractive to the eye.

Out Skerries

The Noup of Noss

NOSS NATIONAL NATURE RESERVE — If one had to recommend a place where the visitor to Shetland, with limited time and travel facilities, could get an impression of the wealth of Shetland's sea-bird population — then it would have to be Noss!

It is not a large island (only 700 acres in extent) but the cliffs at the east side rise to an impressive 592 feet.

Noss lies a short distance from Bressay — the island which shelters Lerwick harbour — and its popularity with sea-birds is no doubt largely due to its geological make-up. On the high east-facing side the sandstone cliff has been eroded and sculpted by weather and time into innumerable ledges and niches which provide ideal nesting platforms for the variety of birds which find food in the rich waters nearby.

Shetland's first Gannet colony became established here in 1911 and has continued to grow to the present total of around 5500 nests. There are also large numbers of Guillemots, Razorbills, Puffins and Kittiwakes. Bonxies and Arctic Skuas nest on the moorland behind the cliffs and as usual there are constant aerial battles being waged over the ownership of food — usually won by the skuas!

Apart from the magnificent sight on the Noup cliffs, the whole island is alive with birds. Oystercatcher, Snipe, Ringed Plover, Rock Dove, Wheatear and Wrens are all common, while the ruinous stone wall round the high parts of the cliffs is a haunt of our only resident finch, the Twite.

The island has a resident staff of warden and boatman in summer and access information can be obtained from the Shetland Tourist Information Office in Lerwick.

The crossing to Noss although short, is subject to weather conditions, and if in doubt the information office would advise.

Noss Sound

The Broch of Mousa

MOUSA — This island lies about half-way between Lerwick and Sumburgh off the east side, and opposite the township of Sandwick. It is a pleasant green island of about 450 acres, used mainly for the grazing of sheep. Although the island has not been inhabited for about a hundred years, there are many ruinous buildings and stone enclosures to be seen. Most of these date from the 17th and 18th centuries when Shetland populations were exceptionally high and many small islands, now abandoned, were tenanted.

But the most famous relic on Mousa is, without doubt, the remains of a broch or fort. A circular stone structure, it still stands over forty feet high and is thought to date back over a thousand years to Celtic or Pictish times.

While this attracts archaeologists and historians, it also has an ornithological interest, because the walls are tenanted by Storm Petrels (as is the boulder beach nearby). Even on day visits you can often hear the birds churring away inside the walls, but it is certainly worthwhile to take advantage of one of the organised boat trips from Broonies Taing in Sandwick, which go out specially at night to see the petrels circle the ancient walls like a living halo.

Apart from the bird interest, and there are lots of skuas, Fulmars, terns, Tysties and others, there is a large tidal pool where seals become trapped at low tide and can be watched — or photographed — at leisure.

FOULA — The name 'Foula' is derived from the old Norse 'Fugl-øy' meaning 'bird-island' and suggests that the importance of the bird population the island has been recognised for a very long time.

Lying out in the open Atlantic Ocean, 14 miles from the nearest point in Shetland, and with only one rather exposed creek suitable for landing from a boat, Foula is one of the most isolated inhabited islands in Britain.

In the past it often featured in national news bulletins when prolonged storms cut the island off from the rest of the world for weeks at a time. Nowadays the establishment of a small airstrip has done much to alleviate the problem of essential supplies. The availability of helicopters belonging to HM Coastguard has lessened the worries of medical emergencies.

Nevertheless Foula remains very much a 'world apart' with a romantic image not shared by any other Shetland island.

Although the human population has declined to a figure of under 40, the bird populations remain impressively large.

The island is only about 3½ miles long, yet on the western side the cliffs rise to a breathtaking 1220 feet above the sea.

All the usual sea-birds are there in numbers which are difficult even to estimate. Puffins, Guillemots, Razorbills, Kittiwakes and Shags abound, and Gannets have colonised the island in the last decade, the increasing population numbered over 200 nests in 1984.

Manx Shearwaters and Storm Petrels inhabit the scree slopes, and Shetland's first breeding Leach's Petrels were confirmed in 1974.

Foula Cliffs

Ham burn, Foula.

On the high moorland the Great Skua population has grown from a few pairs in the middle of last century to a total estimated at over 3000 pairs. It is ironic that this bird which was encouraged because it helped keep the Sea Eagles off the sheep, has expanded to the point where it causes more problems than it solved. But there are signs of a levelling-out in Bonxie populations, and the recent shortages in sandeels has led to massive failures in breeding success. Only time will tell if this is temporary . . .

The first pair of Fulmar to nest in Shetland did so on Foula in 1876, and this sparked off another 'population explosion' which is only now showing some signs of abating, but still leaves Fulmar as the most numerous breeding bird in Shetland.

It takes determined effort — and some cash — to visit Foula, but it is certainly worth the effort!

FAIR ISLE — This magical island lies midway between Shetland and Orkney, 25 miles of often turbulent water lying between it and its nearest neighbours.

It used to take a stomach-turning three hours in the small boat 'Good Shepherd' from Grutness near Sumburgh, but some of us 'old stagers' may feel that some of the glamour went away with the introduction of an island airstrip. Regular flights mean that in only a few minutes flying time from Tingwall you can touchdown on Fair Isle without a trace of the dreaded *mal-de-mer* — but then we don't live on Fair Isle!

It has been long recognised as a place attractive to migrating birds, and that still remains its main interest.

As early as the turn of the century it was known to men like Dr W. Eagle Clarke, who subsequently wrote a book 'Studies in Bird Migration' published in 1912. Others followed in his footsteps, noted ornithologists like Rear-Admiral Stenhouse.

After the last war George Waterston bought the island and established the Fair Isle Bird Observatory in old Naval buildings at North Haven.

Kenneth Williamson was the first warden and director and embarked on an intensive programme of studies, not only on migrants but on many aspects of the local breeding birds.

These studies have continued to the present day under a succession of wardens.

Sheep Rock, Fair Isle.

By 1967 the old naval huts were past their best, and could no longer cope with the numbers of people who wanted to take part in the activities of the Observatory. An appeal was launched and with the help of a number of trusts, government grants and private donors, a fine new observatory was built at a cost of £51,000. This provided comfortable accommodation for up to 24 visitors who took part in all the activities of the observatory.

Extensive refurbishment again became necessary in the last few years and work was completed in 1989, extending the accommodation and installing computer equipment to help organise the massive amount of data accumulated over the years.

A visit to Fair Isle is a memorable experience, not only in order to help in the work of the observatory, but to see how island people live and work, and to get a feel and taste of life on a remote island.

THE PEERIE ISLES —

"Lingey, Daaey, and bonny Hascosay,
Oxna, Papa, Hildasay and Hoy.
Samphrey, Bigga, Brother Isle and Orfasay,
Magic names that even time cannot destroy."

Magic names indeed! Originating in the dawn of Shetland's history, the place names are still a tangible link with our former alliance and allegiance to Scandinavia.

One doesn't need to be an Old Norse scholar to understand the meaning of some of the names of the peerie (i.e. little) islands.

There are over 80 uninhabited 'sheepholms' and small islands around Shetland, ranging in size from a few acres to over 700. While there are many similarities in the bird-life each islet has its individual character.

Let us take a look at a typical 'peerie isle', one called Sound Grüney which lies in the tidal sounds between Yell, Unst and Fetlar. The name means 'the green

Muckle Holm, Yell Sound.

Grüna Stack.

island which lies in the sound' (the sea passage between islands).

It is only about 13 acres in extent which in the past provided summer pastures for about seven cows, the good green grass now grazed by sheep.

Wild flowers such as Lesser Celandine, Vernal Squill, Thrift and Scurvy Grass make successive splashes of colour, but is largely kept in check by the sheep.

It is June and the birds are all busy with nesting duties; as we nose our way carefully towards the beach, keeping an eye out for signs of hidden reefs or shoals, a cloud of Arctic Terns and Black-headed Gulls rise with a clamour. The deep 'oow, oow' of the pair of Great Black-backed Gulls is scarcely audible above the din. Two or three Black Guillemots, necks stretched and tails cocked, swim out of the way of the boat, nervously dipping their beaks as if anxious for their mates sitting on eggs in the small ruined cairn on the island.

We drop anchor off the strangely black-looking beach, and the noise disturbs a couple of Turnstones who fly off with their metallic call. One is obviously in immature plumage, but the other is very smart in chestnut, black and white; we wonder yet again if they might occasionally breed . . .!

The gulls and terns have quietened down and we row ashore in the dinghy, but a pair of Oystercatchers take over. They evidently have young and tell us about it in no uncertain manner.

We crunch our way up the beach, which is of blackish serpentine pebbles with here and there a translucent green stone glistening like a ready-made pendant.

At the top of the beach we nearly trip over a Fulmar which manages to spatter our boots with a mouthful of oil before we dodge clear and leave her muttering imprecations as she settles back on her egg.

A pair of Hooded Crows are flying around looking innocent, but we find their nest on a ledge with five young who snap open vermilion lined beaks when we call "craa".

In a small patch of emergent yellow iris leaves, we spot a sitting Eider Duck in time to circle round to avoid disturbing her. They have a difficult enough time saving their brood of ducklings from the black-backs.

As we walk round the coast a party of scrawny immature Shags leap off the rocks in alarm and alert a couple of Common Seals who assess the situation and decide that 'discretion is the better part . . .' and slip off their rock to re-emerge and follow us from the safety of the sea as we make our way back to the boat.

We note two pairs of Rock Pipits this year, one pair of Wrens, Arctic Terns down a bit but a pair of Lapwing which may have nested . . . Normal fluctuations, no excitement. Just an average little Shetland island, probably much as it has been for generations — and we would like to keep it that way!

RED-THROATED DIVER
(Gavia stellata)

SHET: Rain Gjüs
NOR: Smålom
ICE/FAR: Lómur

The name 'Rain Gjüs' is universal in Shetland nowadays, but judging by the number of small lochs called 'Loomi-shun' (Diver tarn) the Norse name was in former use.

STATUS: Widespread summer resident.

IDENTIFICATION — L: 21'' — 23'' (53-68cm). The smallest of the four diver species and the only one to breed in Shetland.

In flight is recognised from Shag (with which it may be confused) by narrower wings, white underparts, and by the outstretched head and neck which is generally arched downwards.

On the water in poor light the bird appears dark with a white breast showing only at the front. The red throat patch only shows up in good light, contrasting with the light grey head and neck. A good feature in distant views is the angle at which the head and neck are carried; the neck held fairly straight and angled forward, with the beak held slightly uptilted.

Young birds lack the red throat patch and, like adults in winter have the face and neck largely white.

CALL — The call most commonly heard in the breeding season is a harsh 'quacking' flight call, generally given as the bird returns to the sea after a visit to the breeding lochs. Loud wailing display calls are performed on the water, often on the sea but also as a greeting to its mate on a loch or as a territorial warning to another diver.

HABITAT AND DISTRIBUTION — A summer visitor to inshore waters, and to inland lochs large and small. Entirely aquatic, it feeds on small fish such as young saithe and sandeel. Rarely seen after September, although a few have been recorded wintering in recent years.

BREEDING — Always near inland lochs and ponds, the nest is merely an indentation on the bank within a metre of the water, as the 'Rain Gjüs' is highly specialised for diving and is unable to walk efficiently or to get airborne from the land. The two large olive-brown eggs are laid from late May and are incubated for nearly four weeks. The young are fed on small fish which are carried from the sea by both parents.

The young birds go to the sea during August and disperse southward with the adults for the winter. A survey in 1983 suggested a total of about 700 breeding pairs.

GENERAL — A well known and liked local bird, its Shetland name comes from the belief that its calls can foretell the weather. One interpretation is 'Weet ower 'aa, weet ower 'aa', and another states the obvious 'The mair weet the waar (worse) weather'.

A local rhyme says —

When the rain goose goes to the hill,
Tak' doon your boats, go whar' you will.
But when the rain goose goes to the sea,
Pull your boats up in the lee.

A highly specialised and rather vulnerable bird which, if disturbed, leaves the nest open to predation by gulls and skuas.

Hill walkers and loch fishermen in particular should take great care not to disturb this bird which is specially protected by law.

LITTLE GREBE
(Tachybaptus ruficollis)

STATUS: A casual visitor which has bred a few times.

Mainly recorded as a winter visitor to sheltered inshore waters or the richer lochs.

Breeding was suspected at Spiggie Loch as long ago as 1901 (Venables). A pair bred at Hillwell Loch in 1967, and probably also at Sand Water in 1981.

FULMAR
(Fulmarus glacialis)

SHET: Maalie
NOR/FAR: Havhest
ICE: Fýll

STATUS: Widespread common resident.

IDENTIFICATION — L: 18½'' (45-50cm). A stocky, rather gull-like petrel with a short neck and a thick yellowish beak with 'tubed' nostrils. The general colour is white with a grey back and wings. In late summer, adults have a slightly 'dirty' look with a yellowish tinge to the head, while newly fledged young are much 'cleaner' looking.

Quite distinctive in flight, the Fulmar is a superb exponent of the art of gliding. Its stiffly held wings tell it apart from the fairly similar Herring Gulls, as it glides and banks along the cliffs or over the sea.

Occasional birds may be seen which are dark smokey grey all over. These belong to a more northern 'blue' phase. Fulmars regularly follow ships, have difficulty in taking off from flat ground and on the sea patter along the surface some way before becoming airborne.

CALLS — Silent on the wing, Fulmars have a variety of hoarse cackling calls when squabbling on cliff ledges or fighting over food on the sea.

HABITAT AND DISTRIBUTION — Generally pelagic, fulmars spend much of their time on the wing over the sea. Apparently catching most of their food on the sea surface at night, they are nevertheless opportunist feeders and often swarm round fishing boats to pick up discards or offal. They will regularly visit breeding places throughout the year.

BREEDING — As an example of the phenomenal success of this bird, it is recorded that the first pair of Maalies nested in 1876 on Foula, and a count on that island in 1987 showed a total of 46,800 occupied sites.

Fulmars now nest on virtually all Shetland's islands and coastlines.

As well as the traditional cliff ledges site, Fulmars will also nest on steep hillsides, and even in the lee of stone walls or abandoned houses. A single large white egg is laid in any convenient place, sometimes in the abandoned nest of other birds such as Raven. While incubating, the adults will often refuse to leave the egg, defending it by spitting a mouthful of sticky oil at any intruder, be it bird, animal or man.

The egg is incubated for about eight weeks, and the young take about the same time to get to the stage where they can flutter and glide on to the sea. Where the nesting place is some distance from the sea this often leads to the fledgling crash-landing among crops or vegetation from where it has difficulty in extricating itself. Fulmars are long lived birds, seldom breeding until they are eight or nine years old, and having a breeding life of possibly fifty years.

GENERAL — Admired by many people for their boldness and power of flight there is nevertheless a suspicion that their sheer numbers and oil-spitting habits have contributed to the demise of other cliff nesters, in particular the Peregrine Falcon.

MANX SHEARWATER
(Puffinus puffinus)

SHET: Lyrie or Cockasüdie
FAR: Scrápur
ICE: Skrofa
NOR: Havlire

STATUS: A scarce summer breeder.

IDENTIFICATION — L: 14'' (36cm). Only likely to be seen flying over the sea, usually in small parties, the Manx Shearwater looks like a small black and white Fulmar (to which it is related).

It soars and swoops on stiffly held wings, alternately showing black upperparts and white below as it banks and turns. Short glides are interspersed with a few quick wingbeats.

All of the upper parts are sooty black, and the whole of the underparts from chin to tail are white. There is some mottling where the colours join at the neck. The rather long thin beak has a hooked tip. It has the tube nostrils typical of the family, though not so prominent as those of the Fulmar.

CALLS — Normally silent during the day, at night returning birds greet their mates with loud crowing and cackling calls.

HABITAT AND DISTRIBUTION — Entirely pelagic outside the nesting season, there are no large concentrations of breeding Manx Shearwaters in Shetland.

During summer from about mid-May the best places in Shetland to look for them are from headlands such as Sumburgh Head in the south, or Lamba Ness in Unst (but beware other shearwater species).

Lambhoga in Fetlar and the Horse of Burravoe in Yell are good because there are small breeding colonies here and Manx Shearwaters tend to gather inshore in the evenings before relieving their mate on the nest. Also known to breed on Foula and there are suggestions they may have been more widespread formerly.

BREEDING — Manx Shearwaters only approach their nests after dark. Their favourite nesting sites are grassy cliff slopes where the birds can burrow well into the turf to lay their single white egg. Incubation takes up to 54 days and the young is fed in the burrow on various kinds of regurgitated fish for about two months, after which it is abandoned. It will fly about two weeks later.

GENERAL — Anyone wishing to see and hear Manx Shearwaters on their breeding grounds in Shetland, must go out at night during June/August to one of the known sites where they may be rewarded by a weird cacophony of calls and ghostly shapes as birds return to their burrows to change over incubation duties or feed the young.

STORM PETREL
(Hydrobates pelagicus)

SHET: Mootie or Aalamootie
ICE: Stormsvala
FAR: Drunnhvíti
NOR: Havsvale

STATUS: Summer visitor, breeding in large numbers.

IDENTIFICATION — L: 6'' (15cm). This tiny (sparrow-sized) seabird is sometimes seen at sea around Shetland. Flying low over the waves with fluttering erratic wing-beats it looks like a lost House Martin with its sooty-black plumage and white rump patch.

Petrels tend to patter and dabble on the sea surface while feeding. In the hand the tiny beak has the typical tubed nostrils of the family. This feature and the small black webbed feet should make identification easy. But beware of the larger and rarer Leach's Petrel which has a *forked* tail. It also has slower and less fluttery wing-beats. Most petrels exhude a faint musty smell.

CALLS — Silent at sea, Storm Petrels can be heard at night (and occasionally during the day) making a purring noise interrupted by 'hiccup' sounds. This call is usually made underground in the nesting burrows but occasionally a repeated 'chick chick' call will be heard from birds flying round the nesting territory. Leach's Petrel has a louder 'chickerie-ick-chick' call on the breeding grounds.

HABITAT AND DISTRIBUTION — A summer visitor to Shetland cliffs and offshore islands, Storm Petrels are pelagic outside the breeding season and range far over the oceans. Birds ringed in Shetland have been recovered as far away as the Indian Ocean.

Their small size makes them difficult to observe from the shore during the day, but they can sometimes be seen from the ferry boats which serve the outer isles such as Fair Isle and Foula, and they sometimes come to feed on any oily matter around fishing boats offshore.

Due to their nocturnal and secretive nature, numbers and distribution of the small petrels in Shetland is poorly known.

There are a number of well known breeding sites such as the scree cliffs of Fetlar, Foula and Fair Isle and the famous broch on the island of Mousa. At these places the breeding numbers probably run into thousands. Most of the smaller offshore islands have nesting 'Stormies' and Leach's Petrels are known to have small breeding colonies on Foula and Grüney (Ramna Stacks).

BREEDING — Scree and grass slopes in the cliffs are favoured nesting places, but stone walls, boulder beaches and earthy banks along the shores all offer hidden crevices where the single small white egg can be laid. Incubation takes as long as 40 days and the chick is fed in the nest for a further six weeks or so.

They are then abandoned by the parents and leave the nest when about two months old.

By this time the evenings are getting dark and the newly fledged petrels sometimes get confused by bright lights such as pier lights and brightly lit boats — or even Halloween bonfires. They may then become grounded and get caught by cats.

LEACH'S PETREL
(Oceanodroma leucorrhoa)

STATUS: Rare summer breeding visitor.

Suspicions of breeding were confirmed in 1974 when a nest was located on Foula.

Six or seven other occupied burrows were found the following year.

In 1981 a small number were found breeding on Grüney (near Ramna Stacks), there may be others not yet discovered.

For comparisons with Storm Petrel see under that species.

GANNET
(Sula bassana)

SHET: Solan
ICE/FAR: Súla
NOR: Havsule

STATUS: Mainly summer visitor.

IDENTIFICATION —L: 36'' (90cm). There are no problems over identifying this, the largest of our breeding seabirds. Adults have snowy white plumage, offset by a buff head and black wingtips. From the strong 'marlin spike' beak at the front to the pointed tail, the streamlined body is ideally shaped to plunge dive into the sea from a considerable height in order to catch the fish on which it lives.

Young Gannets can be a bit confusing, because their plumage is a dark sooty brown with white flecks. It takes at least four years before they gradually attain full adult colouring. It is difficult to believe that Gannets are related to Shags and Cormorants, but a close look at the feet will show that they share the distinction of having all four toes joined by webs.

CALLS — Breeding Gannets are quite noisy-if not very tuneful-on their nesting grounds; a loud harsh 'aaargh aargh' is the usual call, and at sea they will often give the same call as they swing into the start of a plunge dive.

HABITAT AND DISTRIBUTION — Outside the breeding season Gannets are pelagic, following fish shoals wherever they become available.

They were first recorded breeding in Shetland on Noss about 1911. Another colony became established on Vesta Skerry (near Muckle Flugga in Unst) in 1917, and eventually spread on to the cliffs of Hermaness. Recent counts revealed over 5,200 nests on Noss and over 8,000 on Hermaness.

In more recent years colonies have become established on Fair Isle (nearly 700 nests in 1989) and Foula (over 200 nests in 1984).

BREEDING — Large bulky nests are constructed from seaweed or any available flotsam, and nowadays discarded polypropylene netting is also used. This can be a problem when birds fight for possession and can result in hopeless entanglement and death.

One egg is normal, the dirty white colour being caused by a chalky deposit on the shell. The young at first is clad in white down, but this is soon replaced by the first chocolate brown plumage in which the fledgling flutters or glides onto the sea where it may swim in a southerly direction for weeks before it can fly.

GENERAL — While Gannets have never been used as human food in Shetland, in the 1939-45 war large numbers were shot and sent to London where, it was said, they appeared on the menus of the better restaurants as 'Highland Goose'!

25

First year Cormorants are easy with their white fronts, but second year birds with dark brown backs and pale brown fronts are quite like immature Shags.

Seen together, the difference is that the Cormorant is larger with a thicker neck and heavier beak. In mixed roosts, Cormorants tend to stay farther up on the grass and are almost always the first to fly off when approached.

If birds are seen flying over land or feeding in a fresh water loch or burn, then it is almost certainly a Cormorant, Shags are exclusively marine (unless sick).

Adult Cormorants are quite handsome in breeding plumage with a white spot on the 'thigh' and white throat patch. Seen closely the filamentous white feathers on the head and the bronze 'coat-of-mail' appearance of the back feathers leave no doubts as to the species.

CALLS — Normally silent apart from a guttural 'quarrk' when quarrelling. Nestlings have a squealing call when food-begging.

HABITAT AND DISTRIBUTION — As Cormorants feed almost exclusively on fish they are most often seen in inshore waters or in freshwater lochs where they catch trout and eels. They are mainly resident, and have traditional roost places in winter, usually on grassy slopes near the shore on islands, where they may congregate in small flocks. These roost places are always greener than the surrounding land because of enrichment by droppings.

Around 400 pairs of Cormorants nest in Shetland, and for reasons that are unclear, nearly all of the breeding colonies are on the west side of the Shetland Mainland, in places such as Hillswick, Muckle Roe, Vaila etc. Exceptions were a small colony on Bressay, now extinct, and a recently established colony on Little Holm in Yell Sound.

Sizeable flocks roam around the Yell Sound islands in winter and small numbers can be seen in many coastal areas.

BREEDING — Breeding is usually in colonies on the tops of isolated sea-stacks, cliff edges or on small islets, and the sites are often used year after year. Three or four eggs are laid in a bulky seaweed and grass nest, and the young are fed on regurgitated fish.

CORMORANT
(Phalacrocorax carbo)

SHET: Muckle Scarf, Lorin, Hiplin, (adult), Brongi (immature)
FAR: Hiplingur
ICE: Dílaskarfur
NOR: Storskarv, Kvitlåring

STATUS: Mainly resident.

IDENTIFICATION — L: 36'' (92cm). The 'cormorant shape' is known to most people, and the only confusion likely is with Shag when the birds are immature.

SHAG
(Phalacrocorax aristotelis)

SHET: Scarf
FAR: Scarvur
ICE/SCAN: Toppskarv

STATUS: Resident and widespread around coasts.

IDENTIFICATION — L: 30'' (76cm). The Shag is a smaller, slimmer and more exclusively marine relative of the Cormorant.

Adults are easy to distinguish between January and May because they sport a large recurved crest on the head, have a distinctive yellow gape and a glossy dark green plumage. However they appear black at a distance or in the water. The crest is gradually lost after breeding begins. Young are brownish with paler fronts, sometimes with a white chin-spot.

Shags can sometimes be confused with Red-throated Divers at a distance, but the more curved neck of the Shag and the way it tends to jump almost out of the water when diving (especially in deep water) is diagnostic.

Shags do not normally fly as high as Cormorants, and rarely fly over land.

CALLS — Normally silent, birds on nests will protest with a harsh croaking (and head-shaking threats) if approached.

HABITAT AND DISTRIBUTION — Shags are present in inshore waters the whole year round, and winter movements are largely in response to availability of small fish such as young saithe which form the staple food. At this time Shags will congregate in good fishing areas and act in concert to 'drive' a shoal into shallow water.

BREEDING — Come April, birds tend to congregate in cliffs, geos (clefts) and areas of boulder scree. They usually nest in loose colonies and are more inclined to use cliff ledges (even inside caves) and to place their nests in the shelter of boulders rather than out in the open as Cormorants do. A good place to watch Shags is near the lighthouse on Sumburgh Head. Up to five eggs are laid from late April onwards in a large untidy seaweed nest. The edge of the nest is often decorated with fresh greenery (such as Scurvy Grass) and this is replenished when necessary. The young are fed on regurgitated fish, and a Shag colony usually takes on a distinctive smell!

GENERAL — As with Gannets, thousands of Shags were shipped 'south' in the last war and sold in restaurants as 'Highland Duck'. As well as shooting them during the day, men would go out in boats at night to a known roost, hoist a sail and shine a light to dazzle the birds. The Shags would then fly into the sail and fall in the boat.

In the 'old days' in Shetland, Shags were used as food, and it is recorded that they were caught by setting lines with hooks baited with small saithe.

GREY HERON
(Ardea cinerea)

SHET: Haigrie
FAR: Hegri
NOR: Hegre

STATUS: Winter visitor. Has bred.

A regular winter visitor from Scandinavia which arrives in early autumn. During the winter they can often be seen standing motionless on the shoreline watching for small fish.

When disturbed it flies off with a loud 'frank' call and is quite distinctive in flight with its neck folded back and its broad slow-flapping wings.

Summering individuals are sometimes seen, and breeding has been recorded a couple of times, though not in recent years.

About 1900 a nest was found in the cliffs at Rouska (Fetlar) and they were said to have nested again in a subsequent year (Venables).

One (or more) were said to have nested in the Neap of Foraness (Delting) some time in the 1930s. (C. Laurenson).

There is a small cliff-nesting colony in Orkney.

MUTE SWAN
(Cygnus olor)

STATUS: Vagrant.

A very rare visitor to Shetland although Orkney has a large resident population.

Introduced birds have bred a few times.

The most successful introduction was to the Loch of Spiggie in the early years of the century, when Mr Henderson brought a pair from Orkney. By 1919 there were at least 10 swans on the loch, but all were shot by local lads returning from the First World War (Venables).

WHOOPER SWAN
(Cygnus cygnus)

STATUS: A regular winter visitor.

Every year from the end of September, Whooper Swans from Iceland begin to arrive in Shetland. They build up in numbers on favoured lochs and stay as long as their food supply lasts.

The Loch of Spiggie usually has the largest numbers, as many as 300 having been recorded in a good year.

Occasionally birds which have suffered wing damage will stay on to summer in Shetland.

Venables records that a wounded pair bred on Spiggie from 1905 until the end of the war in 1918. Their young always left with the wintering birds in spring.

With the Mute Swans they were all shot by soldiers returning from the First World War.

GREYLAG GOOSE
(Anser anser)

SHET: Grey Gjüs
FAR: Grágás
ICE: Grágæs
NOR: Grågås

STATUS: Recent colonist in small numbers.

IDENTIFICATION — A typical grey goose, very similar to the old Shetland domesticated species (and probably its ancestral form).

Wild birds are typically slimmer and lighter in weight than the domestic birds. The Greylag is distinguished from other grey geese by the pale grey forewing, seen well in flight and when the bird stretches its wings. The body is grey/brown with lighter margins to the feathers and paler underneath, the beak is orange and the legs and feet are flesh coloured.

CALLS — Indistinguishable from those of the domestic goose.

HABITAT AND DISTRIBUTION — Depending on the weather, every autumn sees a passage of 'grey geese' through Shetland. Severe westerly gales at the time of their normal migration from Iceland to Scotland usually brings flocks which have been displaced in an easterly direction. Most of these — mainly Greylag and Pink-footed Geese — will re-orientate after a few days of rest and continue to their destination, but small numbers often stay on to winter in Shetland.

Heather hills and small crofts are not attractive to geese generally, but the richer farming valleys with large open fields give the birds the food and security they look for.

In the last few years a number of Greylag have stayed on to breed in Shetland, the first documented breeding record was from Unst in 1985, where they now appear to be well established.

These birds are possibly of Icelandic stock, and have been attracted to stay on in Shetland by the establishment of large areas of grassland re-claimed from rough hill pastures. This has been made possible by government aided re-seeding programmes.

BREEDING — So far few nests have been found, but family parties of adults and goslings have regularly appeared in June on the recently re-seeded areas in the north isles of Shetland.

Highest counts from a single area have been of aggregations of nearly thirty goslings, with brood sizes averaging between four and six.

29

SHELDUCK
(*Tadorna tadorna*)

SHET: Links Gjüs
FAR: Tjaldursont
NOR: Gravand

STATUS: Regular breeder in small numbers.

IDENTIFICATION — L: 24'' (60cm). A big handsome duck with a goose-like stance, a dark metallic green head and neck and a bright red bill.

The body is boldly patterned with black, white and chestnut. The sexes are similar except that the female is a bit less contrasty and lacks the red knob on the bill sported by the male.

CALLS — Rather silent generally, females have a quacking 'ak-ak-ak---' when chasing others. The male has a whistling 'whee-oo' display call in the spring.

HABITAT AND DISTRIBUTION — Resident in small numbers, though birds disappear to unknown moulting areas in late autumn, usually re-appearing during December. The Dunrossness area of the south mainland, with its wide sandy beaches and large areas of sand dunes, is their main resort.

They will, however, occur in other areas including offshore islands and there are breeding records from Papa Stour, Unst, Yell and Burra Isle. But numbers in total are small, and probably no more than a dozen pairs breed in Shetland in any year.

BREEDING — Big, noticeable, and not particularly shy they may be, but they become pretty secretive at nesting time. They hide their nest away underground, e.g. in a rabbit burrow or similar, and lay a large clutch of creamy eggs.

Ten or more eggs may be laid, and the ducklings are brought to the shores, often to open sandy beaches where sadly, they are often preyed upon by gulls and skuas.

WIGEON
(*Anas penelope*)

STATUS: Regular winter visitor. Breeds occasionally.

Like most ducks they are secretive about breeding and may be more regular than is suggested.

Venables claimed Wigeon nested on several islands, quoting Saxby who reported fresh eggs from 24th April.

The first positive record was a female with young at Sand Water each year between 1976 and 1978. Breeding was again confirmed at undisclosed sites in central mainland in 1985, 1989 and 1990.

TEAL
(*Anas crecca*)

STATUS: Uncertain, a few may be resident.

A regular winter visitor and passage migrant which breeds regularly in small numbers.

Few nests have been found but broods of ducklings are seen from time to time. Records have come from Dunrossness, Sandwick, Northmavine, Yell, Fetlar and Unst.

MALLARD
(Anas platyrhynchos)

SHET: Stock Deuk
FAR: Villdunna
ICE: Stockönd
NOR: Stokkand

STATUS: Resident and widespread.

IDENTIFICATION — L: 23'' (58cm). A bird which should be familiar to everyone, as it is found all over Britain, often in a semi-domesticated state in town parks and ponds. The male in breeding plumage has a glossy green head and neck, separated from the dark chestnut breast by a narrow white collar. The body can look very pale grey in bright sun, and with a good view, the curled upper tail coverts are characteristic. The wings are darker grey with an iridescent purple/blue speculum.

The female also has the glossy speculum bordered with white, but otherwise the whole plumage is mottled brown and buff.

The male goes into an 'eclipse' plumage between July and September, when he resembles the female.

CALLS — The female has the familiar duck 'quack' and the male has a higher pitched and more subdued version.

HABITAT AND DISTRIBUTION — The Mallard is a bird of marshes and lochs, favouring the richer waters with emergent vegetation.

It is generally a much shyer, wilder bird than its town counterpart and is quite secretive about nesting.

Shetland birds are probably mainly resident and while they are widespread in suitable wet marshy habitat, nowhere can they be said to be abundant. During hard weather in winter Mallard tend to be more obvious as they resort to the shores and the brackish 'houbs' at the heads of voes, or to crofting land to feed on stubble or wet ditches.

BREEDING — The nest is typically near the drier edge of marshes, often under long vegetation such as Soft Rush (*Juncus effusis*). Ten or even a dozen eggs are laid, and they are incubated by the female alone, hatching in about 28 days. Broods of ducklings have been recorded as early as April, and as late as September.

GENERAL — The Mallard has long been a favourite quarry for sportsmen and 'pot-shooters', but the practice has died out in many parts of Shetland.

Probably more damage is done to Mallard numbers by Hooded Crows (and to a lesser extent by gulls and skuas). Crows can terrorise breeding marshes, one will lure the female duck into a chase while the other picks off the ducklings.

PINTAIL
(Anas acuta)

STATUS: Sporadic and uncommon.

This handsome duck has bred a number of times in the Dunrossness district (Venables). Summering birds recorded in other areas but the only recent breeding record was also from Dunrossness in 1977.

SHOVELER
(Saptula clypeata)

STATUS: Irregular visitor to the richer lochs where it may overwinter at times.

The only regular breeding haunt is the Loch of Hillwell in Dunrossness, where successful nesting was first recorded in 1953 and 1954 (Venables). Family parties have been recorded there most years with three pairs in 1982. Breeding has also been recorded from the nearby Loch of Spiggie, several times at Sand Water, and Fetlar where two pairs nested in 1990.

TUFTED DUCK
(Aythya fuligula)

FAR: Trøllont
NOR: Toppand
ICE: Skúfönd

STATUS: Mainly a winter visitor. Probably a few resident.

IDENTIFICATION — L: 17'' (43cm). The bold contrast of the white flanks with the wholly black body, makes the male unmistakable. A long backward-drooping crest is not always obvious if the bird is diving. The female is dark brown with variable paler markings on the underside, and can be confused with female Scaup. The female Tufted Duck can show a variable amount of white at the base of the bill, but it is never as extensive or 'clean' as that on female Scaup.

Both male and female show a white wing-bar in flight, and the male in 'eclipse' plumage resembles the female.
CALLS — Seldom heard. The male has a soft whistle and the female a low growling 'kurr kurr'.

HABITAT AND DISTRIBUTION — Winter flocks of up to 100 or more as well as smaller parties, can be found on many of the richer lochs. They may resort to the sea in a hard winter when the freshwater lochs freeze over. Wintering birds tend to leave during April. A large moult flock can usually be seen on the Loch of Clickimin between July and September.
BREEDING — A fairly recent colonist, initially nesting only in the West Mainland. It now breeds regularly in a few other places such as the lochs in the Tingwall valley, Dunrossness and occasionally in other islands such as Vementry and Unst, but total numbers are small.

It nests among long vegetation not far from water and favours the security offered by little islands.

The greenish eggs number from six upwards and are usually laid in late May or June, hatching in about 24-26 days.

The young are tended by the female and can dive efficiently and catch food within a day or two of hatching.

EIDER
(Somateria mollissima)

SHET: Dunter
FAR: Æda
ICE: Æður
NOR: Ærfugl

STATUS: Resident and widespread.

IDENTIFICATION — L: 23'' (58cm). A large chunky sea-duck, the drakes boldly patterned in black and white and the females dark brown. The head shape of Eider alone is usually enough to confirm the species. The forehead is long and sloping and the beak continues the profile to a fairly narrow tip.

Drakes are in full plumage from October through until late June, when the upperparts are predominately white except for the black top to the head, a sea-green patch on the nape and a variable rosy suffusion on the upper breast. Underparts, wings and tail are black with the exception of a white thigh patch.

Females are generally warm brown, closely barred and mottled darker. Immature birds resemble the female at first, but young males in their 2nd and 3rd year can show varied patterns of browns, often with white upper breasts.

In 'eclipse' plumage the males gradually change to a patchy dark brown with some white on the wings, and are flightless for a time in late summer.

CALLS — Can be quite noisy in display, males often calling in concert, a musical 'aah-oo' and females responding with a deeper 'kuk-kuk'. Small young have a high pitched cheeping call.

HABITAT AND DISTRIBUTION — Thoroughly marine outside breeding season and widely dispersed round the coastal areas, Shetland birds are believed to be resident. Males have specific moulting areas where they form dense flocks. This is usually near remote headlands and skerries. Only when the moult is completed about the end of September do the birds return, sometimes many miles, to the communal winter resorts.

Winter flocks congregate over sandy sea-beds where they dive to over 100 feet at times, to feed on molluscs and crabs. In spring the flocks break up and disperse to breeding places.

BREEDING — The males choose the nesting sites, which may be above the tide line on a beach or farther inland, and then leave the females to make a scrape which is warmly lined with her own down. Five large greenish eggs is the normal clutch, and they hatch in about 28 days. The female usually walks the ducklings to the sea within a day or so of hatching, but if the nest is some way inland near a loch they may stay on the freshwater for a week or two.

GENERAL — After a population peak in the 1970s, (c. 16,500 in 1977) there has been a serious decline in numbers.

Surveys in 1990 estimated a total population of not more than 9,000. The reasons are not obvious, but increased predation on the young by gulls and skuas may be contributary.

33

COMMON SCOTER
(Melanitta nigra)

STATUS: Winter and summer visitor in small numbers.

A few birds are recorded in inshore waters during the winter months with an increase in spring. A regular but tiny breeding population usually visit freshwater lochs from the end of April.

First recorded by Baxter and Rintoul in 1911 from the Walls district, where breeding is still recorded occasionally.

Yell has a few regular pairs, mainly in the south part of the island. Pre-breeding parties are often seen on the Loch of Littlester during May and June. The females then disappear to breeding places where they are very secretive.

There are occasional breeding records from other islands.

VELVET SCOTER
(Melanitta fusca)

STATUS: A winter and spring visitor in very small numbers.

The only record of possible breeding was in 1945 when Venables saw a pair with four well-grown young in Whiteness Voe.

RED-BREASTED MERGANSER
(Mergus serrator)

SHET: Herald
FAR: Toppont
ICE: Toppönd
NOR: Siland

STATUS: Resident and fairly common.

IDENTIFICATION — L: 23'' (58cm). A slim, long-necked, thin-billed diving duck whose style is more akin to Shags or grebes — or even divers — than to the ducks to which group it belongs.

The males in spring are handsome and distinctive birds, with their glossy green head and neck and a prominent, if wispy, crest. A bold white neck ring separates a chestnut spotted breast and a dark back. The upper part of the wing is mainly white with delicately black scalloped edgings to the upper coverts.

The beak and the feet are red.

The female is clad in shades of brown, lighter underneath and with a chestnut tinge on the neck. Her crest is not so prominent. Mergansers are fish eaters and expert divers, slipping under the water more like grebes.

They are shy and suspicious, difficult to approach closely and always ready to take flight (when the white wing patches show up well). Males begin to moult into their 'eclipse' plumage as early as April, which means that summer visitors to Shetland are unlikely to see a drake 'Herald' in full regalia.

CALLS — Normally silent except when courting. Then the males have a ritual display where the head is first pointed upwards then bounced down on the water when the short creaking call can be heard. At the same time the black edged white feathers on the wing coverts are briefly fanned out — but you have to be quick to see it!

HABITAT AND DISTRIBUTION — Almost

entirely marine outside the breeding season, mergansers prefer the sheltered waters of the voes and wicks and are resident as far as is known, though we may get some immigration in winter. Numbers are never large, but in favoured places such as in Sullom Voe concentrations of 50 or so are not uncommon.

BREEDING — The nest is very well hidden away, often near a stream and usually under a bank or in tall vegetation.

A large clutch of eggs is laid and broods of 18 ducklings have been recorded. They are brought down to the sea shortly after hatching and are looked after by the female while they learn to catch small fish.

WHITE-TAILED EAGLE
(Haliaeëtus albicilla)

SHET: Erne
ICE: Haförn
FAR/NOR: Havørn

STATUS: Extinct.

The last pair of Ernes to nest in Shetland had their eyrie at the Neaps of Graveland (Yell) in 1910. The eggs were robbed by a clergyman from England. Sea Eagles had been in decline for many years, five pairs were nesting in the 1890s.

Most nests were on high cliffs or sea-stacks but there is a record of a nest on a small holm in Mousa Water (Walls).

HEN HARRIER
(Circus cyaneus)

STATUS: One old breeding record.

A casual visitor to Shetland although it breeds in Orkney. The only record of former breeding was from the middle of last century. Saxby said he had found a nest with four eggs in tall heather in Yell.

SPARROWHAWK
(Accipiter nisus)

STATUS: Vagrant. Extinct as a breeder.

Saxby (1852) claimed that a few pairs

were breeding during his time in Unst. The nests were mainly on grassy cliff ledges. There have been no breeding records this century and the bird is a passage migrant which regularly winters in the area of the Kergord plantations.

KESTREL
(Falco tinnunculus)

STATUS: Regular migrant. Extinct as a breeder.

Nowadays a migrant to Shetland. Saxby,

Evans & Buckley, and Raeburn all recorded the bird as a regular breeding species.

Said to have nested on cliffs or on steep hillsides. The latest recorded breeding was in 1905 when G. W. Russell found a nest on the bank of a burn near Dales Voe.

MERLIN
(Falco columbarius)

SHET: Peerie Hawk
ICE: Smyrill
FAR: Smyril
NOR: Dvergfalk

(Place names in Shetland such as Smirlees Hill and Smerla Water confirms

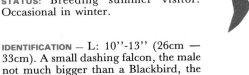

that the Norse name, though no longer known, was used in the past).

STATUS: Breeding summer visitor. Occasional in winter.

IDENTIFICATION — L: 10''-13'' (26cm — 33cm). A small dashing falcon, the male not much bigger than a Blackbird, the Merlin is now our only regular breeding bird of prey. Often seen in hot pursuit

of a Skylark, Meadow Pipit or Wheatear.

The smaller male bird has a slate blue back and rusty streaked underparts, and a slaty tail with a black band near the end.

The female and immatures have a brown streaked back, heavily streaked underparts and a barred tail.

At rest the Merlin sits upright, sometimes on a telegraph pole, a peat stack or other eminence, but always ready to go into action if a suitable prey species is spotted.

CALLS — Normally silent outside the breeding season, when both of the pair will react to an invasion of their territory with a screaming 'keek-eek-eek-eek' while flying round above an intruder. The male's call is usually higher pitched.

HABITAT AND DISTRIBUTION — As a breeding bird, Merlins are thinly spread, mainly over the higher hills and moorlands.

Those occasionally seen during winter months may include birds from more northern areas such as Iceland. In winter Merlins will hunt over the crofting areas and along the shores, there being little in the way of suitable prey in the hills at this time. Shetland ringed juveniles are sometimes trapped in Fair Isle in autumn, suggesting that they head south for the winter.

BREEDING — Regular censusing shows that up to thirty pairs may establish breeding territories in Shetland.

These are typically in areas of heather covered hillsides, occasionally in low cliffs or on man-made structures such as power poles. For several years a pair nested on the aerial support tower of the telephone exchange near Mid Yell.

Three to five reddish brown eggs are nearly always laid in the disused nest of a Hooded Crow, and hatch in about 30 days.

The young are fed on small birds usually caught by the male and delivered to the female who feeds the brood.

GENERAL — Breeding numbers were low in the late 1970s and early 1980s and analysis of addled eggs showed depressingly high levels of contamination with the chemical Dieldrin.

PEREGRINE
(Falco peregrinus)

SHET: Stock Hawk
FAR: Ferdafalkur
NOR: Vandrefalk

STATUS: Declining to near extinction.

Sadly this bird must now be recorded as a former breeder because in 1991 no nesting pairs were located in Shetland.

The decline which became evident in the 1950s, was halted in mainland Britain with the banning of certain chemical pesticides. Shetland Peregrines, which were exclusively coastal, had to share their habitat with an ever increasing Fulmar population and this, coupled with pesticides picked up from eating seabirds, may have prevented recovery and brought the bird to the present state of local extinction.

RED GROUSE
(*Lagopus lagopus*)

FAR: Heiðarýpa
NOR: Lirype

STATUS: Introduced. Resident on mainland Shetland.

IDENTIFICATION — L: 13''-15'' (33cm-38cm). The only member of the grouse family likely to be seen in Shetland.

The characteristic 'chicken' shape, dark red-brown plumage and the bright red combs over the eye (bigger in males) should make identification easy.

Flight is direct and fast, with quick wing-beats interspersed with long glides on bowed wings.

Pheasants have been introduced from time to time and a female of this species could be mistaken for a grouse, though its larger size and pointed tail should be obvious.

Partridge have also been introduced, though they don't usually survive for long, and they are much smaller than grouse.

CALLS — Can be quite noisy at breeding time; a crowing 'kok-ok-ok', ending with a characteristic 'go-bak, go-bak, go-bak'.

HABITAT AND DISTRIBUTION — The Red Grouse is a bird confined to the heather covered uplands and moors of the mainland of Shetland, from Cunningsburgh in the south to Mangaster in the north, including the west mainland. In winter small coveys may visit and feed in the 'outrun' areas of the crofting or farming districts.

Red Grouse were introduced into Shetland by landlords 'for sporting purposes' and it is understood several introductions were made during the 19th century. A number were introduced into Yell early in this century and nests were seen, but the birds apparently died out. There are still occasional reports of birds seen in Yell, and a female with young was reported in 1987. These and birds seen in Unst are presumably birds which have spontaneously crossed from Mainland.

All of the grouse habitat is grazed by sheep, and the heather rarely grows to a height ideal for grouse. This may be the main factor inhibiting population growth, although ground predators such as stoats and feral ferrets may also take eggs and young. The birds remain thinly spread.

BREEDING — The nest is usually among long heather, and may contain up to a dozen eggs. The young are looked after by the female and can fly in about two weeks.

QUAIL
(*Coturnix coturnix*)

STATUS: Sporadic and uncommon.

A summer visitor which has probably bred many times. It is difficult to prove

breeding with this secretive species, but nests are found from time to time when cutting crops. There have been no recent breeding records though calling males have been recorded from several places in potential breeding habitat. The last year when birds were widely reported was 1989.

PHEASANT
(*Phasianus colchicus*)

STATUS: Introduced. Scarce.

Pheasants have been introduced (or have

escaped) a number of times. They have bred 'in the wild' at Kergord and perhaps other places, but conditions are pretty marginal and the feral birds die out after a while.

Birds have been seen recently at Kergord, Tresta and Unst.

CORNCRAKE
(*Crex crex*)

STATUS: Now rare in Shetland.

Formerly a widespread breeding summer visitor to Shetland, Corncrakes have suffered the same decline here as they have done over most of their range.

It is now seldom heard in once popular

haunts such as the Dunrossness area, the Tingwall Valley, Baltasound in Unst and Fetlar. The last good year with a number of calling birds was 1978 but breeding was recorded in Bressay in 1981. Attempted to breed in Unst 1985.

MOORHEN
(Gallinula chloropus)

STATUS: Regular breeder in small numbers.

The first record was in 1890 from 'near Spiggie'. Lowland lochs with well vegetated margins are the preferred habitat. Nesting has been recorded from the Loch of Hillwell, the Brow marshes, Culswick marsh, Sand Water, Tingwall, Strand and Norwick. Birds may winter round crofts in many areas.

COOT
(Fulica atra)

STATUS: Scarce migrant, winter visitor and uncommon breeder.

An exceptional influx was noted in October 1976 when a maximum of 186 were counted on the Loch of Spiggie. Wintering birds often resort to the shores. One hundred years ago 'a fair number' were recorded as nesting at the Loch of Hillwell (Venables) and that remains the only regular nesting place today. Occasional breeding has been recorded at other sites such as Tingwall Loch and Sand Water.

OYSTERCATCHER
(Haematopus ostralegus)

SHET: Shalder
ICE/FAR: Tjaldur
NOR: Tjeld

STATUS: A common summer visitor. Few in winter.

IDENTIFICATION — L: 17'' (43cm). The 'fowl wi' the red neb' needs little in the way of introduction. Noisy and extrovert, the Shalder is a familiar bird in Shetland. Its pied black and white plumage and long red bill sets it apart from any other species. The head, neck and upperparts are glossy black, and there is a broad white wing band. Underparts and tail are white with a broad black terminal band on the tail. The legs and feet are pink. Young birds have greyish legs and a dark base to the bill, and in winter they all develop a white half-collar.

The powerful beak is used to dislodge limpets and to open mussels and other bivalves on which it traditionally fed.

In recent years they have been feeding a lot more in fields for worms and other grubs.

Just occasionally an albino turns up, and gets everyone reaching for the telephone!

CALLS — The usual note is a loud liquid 'kle-ep kle-ep' and this can vary and run into a veritable chorus when a party of birds are displaying.

HABITAT AND DISTRIBUTION — The majority of our Shalders are summer visitors, although a few stay on through the winter, usually in the south of Shetland in the Virkie area, and near Clickimin (Lerwick) and Scalloway. Only scattered birds are seen farther north.

Breeding birds return to Shetland during February. Non-breeding birds (and probably also failed breeders) gather into flocks in late summer, and most have departed by September. A change in habits has been noted all over the species range including the Faroe Islands, where it is the national bird. Birds have moved to inland fields and parkland and usually to areas grazed by sheep, whose shed wool can litter the ground. As a result Oystercatchers are often seen with their legs entangled in tufts of wool. After a time this can become so tightly bound that the blood supply is cut off and the leg or toes lost. If both legs are affected the bird may die.

Although Oystercatchers seem particularly prone to this, other parkland birds such as Lapwings and Curlew can also be affected.

BREEDING — Although eggs have been seen in late April, most birds lay in May. The normal clutch of three are light grey or stone with numerous spots and marks of a darker colour.

The nest is merely a scrape, with a few bits of grass and perhaps pebbles. In former times it was almost exclusively situated on shingle beaches or gravel patches, but nowadays it is just as likely to be in the middle of a grass park or even a ploughed field.

RINGED PLOVER
(*Charadrius hiaticula*)

SHET: Saandy-loo
FAR: Svarthálsa
ICE: Sandlóa
NOR: Sandlo

STATUS: Widespread and mainly resident.

IDENTIFICATION — L: 7½ " (19cm). A small (Starling sized) wader with a grey/brown back, white underparts and strikingly bold black bands across the breast and head. Easy enough to spot when a party are feeding along a sandy beach, but among rocks and pebbles the cryptic markings can cause the bird to 'disappear' into its background. There are only minor differences between the sexes and the fledged young are smudged versions of the adult. The legs and feet are orange.

CALLS — The usual call is a soft melodious 'tiu-eet'. The display 'song' uttered in flight as the bird flies round with exaggerated wing beats, is a repeated 'coo-li-loo, coo-li-loo'.

HABITAT AND DISTRIBUTION — Probably some are resident, but there may be interchange where local birds move south and are replaced by others of more northerly origins in winter. Will associate with other waders such as Turnstones in winter, spending much of the time on sandy or shingly shorelines or on grassland near the sea. Common throughout Shetland in suitable habitats, though nowhere numerous. A 1984 census gave the local breeding population as between 800 and 1,000 pairs.

Breeding birds are usually on territory from early March.

BREEDING — Its chosen nesting territories are sand or gravelly low ground, usually near the shores but will also use disturbed ground such as quarries or the spoil from recent roadworks.

Its nest is usually placed to take advantage of natural camouflage, and is merely a depression in the ground lined with small pebbles, bits of shells etc.

Egg-laying is occasionally recorded in late April but is usually in May. The eggs, usually four in number, are finely dark spotted on a light stone or grey background, and are almost invisible from a few yards away.

The small young are also coloured in shades of grey and white to aid their protective camouflage.

GOLDEN PLOVER
(Pluvialis apricarius)

SHET: Plivver
FAR: Lógv
ICE: Heiðlóa
NOR: Heilo

STATUS: Widespread breeding and winter visitor.

IDENTIFICATION — L: 11'' (28cm). Seen in flocks on open grassy fields, the birds are rather shy of approach, and appear a sort of golden-brown in colour, lighter underneath. They have an upright stance and when feeding will stand motionless for a time then make a short run to pick up something from the ground.

When flocks are gathering in spring, before migrating to breeding grounds, a proportion will be developing the blackish breast which extends upward to include the 'face'.

The intensity of this dark 'shirt-front' varies according to the state of moult and also with the latitude at which birds breed. In general, the 'farther north the darker' is a rough guide. Birds which show a really black face joined to the black breast and outlined in white, are usually birds on their way to breeding grounds in the far north of Scandinavia or Iceland.

Seen really closely the upperparts are beautifully spangled in golden yellow and black.

CALLS — On the breeding grounds the call is often the first indication of the bird's presence. A monosyllabic short whistling 'tuui' will reveal the bird watching from a hummock.

In display plovers fly high, and with exaggerated slow wing-beats will call 'tui-peeo' repeated and interspersed with a yodelling 'tui pee-lo-wi, pee-lo-wi'. A very typical spring sound of the Shetland moorlands.

HABITAT AND DISTRIBUTION — Post-breeding flocks of Golden Plovers gather on grassy pastures and may linger on through to November. It is not easy to evaluate whether these are local birds or immigrants from abroad — possibly both.

If the winter is mild some birds may stay on throughout, but there is always a spring build up. In the month of March there may be flocks of plovers on the fields, still not fully moulted, while breeding birds are already displaying on upland territories. These spring flocks may be birds from northern areas where breeding is later.

Breeding populations are disturbed widely, mainly over the heather covered hills and uplands.

BREEDING — Nests are usually on short heather, though sometimes in peat-moss or grassy pastures. Four eggs are the normal full clutch and, as is usual among waders, they are cryptically coloured to match their surroundings.

The young are active within a short time of hatching, and are beautifully marked with brown and gold to blend with their surroundings.

LAPWING
(Vanellus vanellus)

SHET: Peewit or Tieves Nacket
FAR: Vípa
ICE: Vepja
NOR: Vipe

STATUS: Widespread summer breeder. May winter.

IDENTIFICATION — L: 12'' (30cm). A very distinctive member of the plover family; on the ground with its dark above and white below plumage, and the long curved crest on its head. Seen closely the dark back is an iridescent glossy green with glints of bronze. In flight it is even more distinctive, with broad rounded wings and relatively slow flapping 'wobbly' action. A dark band covers the upper breast, the sides of the head are white. The white tail has a black end and the under-tail coverts are chestnut.

CALLS — These are just as distinctive as the bird. In display the male rises up in the air and then plunges earthward, twisting and turning and calling a shrill 'pee-weet, wiroo-wiroo peee-weet'. This can be repeated many times. The ordinary call is a wheezy 'pee-weet'.

HABITAT AND DISTRIBUTION — The Lapwing loves cultivated, arable and farmland pastures, and outside the breeding season often gathers into large flocks. It has little inclination for the shores though it will feed on coastal grasslands.

It is widely distributed in Shetland. Post breeding flocks will linger on to November but will move out if the weather gets very cold and snowy. A few birds will sometimes stay on through a mild winter, and there is an obvious return movement from February, with birds on breeding territories from early March.

BREEDING — Lapwings prefer the rough-grazing parks, and croft 'outruns' for nesting purposes, building a shallow nest cup which is lined with grasses. Four eggs are normal. They are typical pointed-at-one-end plover eggs, well camouflaged with spots and blotches in shades of brown on a clay-coloured background. The young have only a suggestion of a crest and are mottled grey and white.

41

DUNLIN
(Calidris alpina)

SHET: Plivver's Page
FAR: Fjallmurra
ICE: Lóupræll
NOR: Myrsnipe

STATUS: A common summer breeding visitor.

IDENTIFICATION – L: 7'' (18cm). This small wader is a bird which has different character depending on where you live.

If you are a coastal bird-watcher in England or parts of Scotland, the Dunlin is a brown-above and white-below bird of the mud and sand estuaries in winter, very gregarious and often occurring in huge flocks.

In Shetland it is a solitary bird of the heather moorland with a trilling call, a rich brown marked back and a black tummy-patch. The longish beak has a slight droop at the tip which is sometimes a necessary identification point if the bird is a youngster or in winter plumage and therefore lacking the distinctive black belly-patch.

CALLS – Usual call if flushed is a rather nasal 'zreep' and the display 'song' is a long purring trill.

HABITAT AND DISTRIBUTION – Outside the breeding season it is a bird of the muddy or sandy shores, often in parties but seldom in flocks in Shetland. The Pool of Virkie is one of the favourite haunts for the Dunlin when post-breeding parties gather or birds are on migration through Shetland.

Very few stay on through the winter, and spring passage is not usually remarkable. Returning breeding birds usually stay around the shores for a week or two after arrival in late April, and this is when much display and 'singing' takes place.

BREEDING – The Plivver's Page gets its Shetland name from its habit of following Golden Plover. When the plover is flying high in display flight over the moors, it is sometimes closely followed by the much smaller Dunlin. They share much the same nesting habitat of rough grass and heather moorland.

The nest of the Dunlin is always hidden in a clump of grass, and is a deep cup lined with grasses. The four brown spotted eggs are surprisingly large for this small wader and are laid from mid-May.

There are no figures for overall breeding numbers, but wardens' estimates for reserve populations give examples e.g. Hermaness 33 pairs, Lumbister 35 pairs, Noss 10 pairs (1988).

SNIPE
(Gallinago gallinago)

SHET: Snippik or Horse-gowk
FAR: Mýrisnípa
ICE: Hrossagaukur
NOR: Enkeltbekkasin or Mekregauk

STATUS: Resident and winter visitor.

IDENTIFICATION – L: 10½'' (27cm) of which the bill is 2½'' (6cm).

Snipe are secretive birds, preferring to feed in wet meadows among long grass or rushes, and to hide rather than fly. But when flushed it 'explodes' from the

ground with a harsh 'scraap' and flies with a jerky zig-zag flight to drop suddenly into cover again. Occasionally they will feed out in the open among wet grass or even in cast-up seaweed on the shore. Then the combination of the richly marked brown body and the long straight bill makes identification straightforward. But beware the smaller Jack Snipe which is a migrant and winter visitor in small numbers. It has a shorter bill, and usually flies without making any call. The rare Great Snipe is bigger, has a more direct

flight and, like the Jack Snipe is usually silent.

CALLS — The harsh alarm call is heard at any time of the year, but in spring, part of the mating display of the male is to sit on a prominent vantage point such as a fence post and call, a repeated loud 'chip-pa chip-pa chip-pa', often heard at dusk.

The other sound made by the Snipe is not vocal, but is a 'drumming' noise made by the birds' extended outer tail feathers. As the bird flies round its territory every so often the circular flight is interrupted by a steep swoop during which the 'drumming' noise, which lasts only a few seconds can be heard.

HABITAT AND DISTRIBUTION — Our breeding birds are widespread in suitable habitat and are probably resident. They are augmented in autumn by incoming migrants which usually move on before the onset of winter.

Snipe are active at dusk and on moonlit nights, marshes and wet ditches are favoured feeding grounds. In snowy weather they will resort to the shores.

There are no figures for total breeding numbers, but wardens' reports have estimates for some areas e.g. Hermaness 45 pairs in 1989. Lumbister (Yell) 75 pairs 1990.

BREEDING — Display can be seen and heard from early March, and eggs have been recorded as early as 14th April. The breeding season is protracted and small young have been seen as late as September.

The nest is well hidden under grass or sedges, and the four eggs are blotched in shades of brown.

WOODCOCK
(Scolopax rusticola)

STATUS: Mainly a late autumn migrant. Occasional in winter.

There are records of occasional breeding.

Saxby gives an account of a nest found by the shepherd on Hermaness, in the last century, and an adult with a small chick was seen on Lambhoga (Fetlar) in 1952. C. Inkster, the RSPB Watcher, was shown a nest in Yell in the 1930s.

BLACK-TAILED GODWIT
(Limosa limosa)

STATUS: Passage migrant. One or two pairs breed.

Breeding has been recorded regularly in

the North Isles since 1948, never more than two pairs in any year.

They are believed to be of the Icelandic race *L. l. islandica*. They like extensive tracts of undisturbed marshy ground and are rather sensitive to disturbance.

Otherwise a scarce spring and autumn migrant.

WHIMBREL
(Numenius phaeopus)

SHET: Peerie Whaap or Tang Whaap
FAR: Spógvi
ICE: Spói
NOR: Småspov

In parts of the north isles both Whimbrel and Curlew are called Spooi.

STATUS: A regular and increasing summer breeder.

IDENTIFICATION — L: 15-16'' (38-41cm). Bill 3½'' (9cm).

The only bird in Shetland with which the Whimbrel may be confused is the Curlew. When seen together the smaller size, shorter bill and striped head pattern of the Whimbrel are usually quite distinctive. The tittering whistling call is also diagnostic.

In flight the Whimbrel has quicker wingbeats and, especially on breeding territory tends to hold its head higher, with the beak more horizontal than Curlew.

It is normally much less wary than Curlew and will allow a closer approach. It is also less inclined to feed among long coarse grass and 'inbye' land, preferring the more tundra-like short vegetation of the sheep-grazed uplands.

The general colouration of both birds is light brown with darker streaks, the belly is paler with fewer streaks.

The white rump is noticeable in flight, (there is a Shetland record of the North American race *N.p. hudsonicus* which has a dark rump.)

The head pattern of the Whimbrel comprises a broad pale eyestripe and a dark brown crown which also has a pale stripe up the middle. The Curlew has a streaked brown head, with only a suspicion of a pale 'eyebrow' on some birds.

CALLS — The usual call away from breeding places is a liquid tittering call of six or seven repeated notes. (One of the old names for the Whimbrel is 'seven-whistler'). The courtship calls, delivered in flight starts off like the Curlew's long-drawn 'coourlee, coourlee' etc. but ending in a long-drawn series of 'tittering' whistles. Alarm calls near the nest is a harsher chattering version of the same call.

HABITAT AND DISTRIBUTION — A summer breeding visitor, usually appearing from mid/late April and departing during August with few records after mid September (although there is a recent record of a bird wintering in Unst).

Recent census work has put the Shetland breeding numbers at over 400 pairs, with the largest concentrations in Unst (102 territories) and Fetlar (84 territories).

BREEDING — Unlike Curlew, the Whimbrel likes the short stunted vegetation of the drier hills. The nest is a mere scrape with little lining, and the four pointed eggs are boldly marked on a paler background. Laying takes place in the second half of May or early June and incubation takes 24 days.

CURLEW
(Numenius arquata)

SHET: Whaap
FAR: Tangspógvi
NOR: Storspove

STATUS: Resident and widespread.

IDENTIFICATION — L: 19-25'' (48-63cm).
Bill about 5'' (13cm) the female's
longest.

A big noticeable bird of the grass parks
and re-seeded pastures, the long
downcurved bill unlike most other birds
normally seen in Shetland (but see under
Whimbrel).

At a distance the plumage is overall
pale brown, and the flight is somewhat
like that of a smaller gull or skua. Seen
closely the plumage is streaked and
mottled all over, and the legs are greenish
grey.

Whaaps (whaups if you live in Yell!)
are quite wary birds, spotting people a
long way off and usually taking flight
with the familiar call.

CALLS — Apart from the whistling 'cour-
lee' alarm call, there is the courtship
'song' which is a longer lasting variation
on the same theme, and a harsher
'annoyed' version to warn intruders
away from the young.

HABITAT AND DISTRIBUTION — The Shetland
population is probably largely resident,
spending the winter in the parks and
grassland near crofts and farms. The
resident birds of a district will usually all
move out, often to an offshore island, to
roost for the night (over a thousand have
been noted flighting into Mousa to roost).
Large autumn and spring aggregations
are seen in many areas, sometimes
containing hundreds of birds, but it is not
clear what proportion of these flocks may
be passage migrants.

During snowy spells birds will move
to the coast to feed and in prolonged bad
weather many will leave Shetland.

BREEDING — No estimates of overall
breeding numbers are available, and
wardens' reports again give details of a
few specific areas, e.g. in 1990 the Fetlar
breeding population was estimated at 78
pairs, and the Lumbister Reserve at 15
pairs.

Birds will be on territory and flight
singing heard during April, with eggs laid
during the first part of May. Young birds
will be seen by the end of that month, and
post-breeding families in June.

REDSHANK
(Tringa totanus)

SHET: Ebb-cock or Kjoorlie
FAR/ICE: Stelkur
NOR: Rødstilk

STATUS: Increased breeding numbers in recent years.

IDENTIFICATION — L: 11'' (28cm). A medium sized grey/brown wader with long red legs and a panicky, excitable nature, the Redshank has become increasingly common throughout Shetland as a breeding bird.

On the breeding grounds it can be irritatingly obvious, keeping up a constant yelping for as long as a person is in sight. Outside the breeding season it is a bird of the seashores and nearby pastures.

A conspicuous flight pattern shows a white rump extending in a point up the back, and a prominent white bar along the trailing edge of the wing. In breeding plumage the body, head and neck are a warmer grey/brown with a lot of fine streaking, and the dark beak has a reddish base.

CALLS — The ordinary call is a musical tri-syllabic 'tu-lu-lu' and the display song is a yodelling adaptation of this. The alarm call on the breeding grounds is a harsher single repeated 'chup, chup, chup'.

HABITAT AND DISTRIBUTION — Formerly mainly a passage and winter visitor, Redshanks began to expand their breeding range in Shetland shortly after the last war and spread rapidly. Now nearly all suitable marshy areas resound to the excited yelping of breeding 'Kjoorlies'.

Although it is impossible to separate local birds from passage migrants, there is an obvious spring movement, with a build up of birds from about mid-February. Breeding birds will be on territory about the middle of March.

In late summer there is a post breeding build up of birds from about mid-July, when flocks of over a hundred will collect in favoured feeding areas, mainly along the shores and estuaries.

BREEDING — The nest is usually well hidden in a grass tussock in wet meadows or marshes. Four eggs laid in mid-May make up the usual clutch, and incubation takes about three weeks.

Parent birds often sit on a fence post (or even power pole if one is available) from where it is easier to keep an eye on the small young as they forage among the long grass and sedges.

GREENSHANK
(Tringa nebularia)

STATUS: Fairly regular migrant. Recent breeding.

Saxby recorded that he flushed a Greenshank off four eggs in May 1871, but we had to wait over a hundred years for the next breeding record! A pair were seen with small young in 1980.

They built up to at least seven pairs in 1985, after which they dropped off again. In 1990 there were birds present at three sites.

COMMON SANDPIPER
(Actitis hypoleucos)

STATUS: Passage migrant and annual breeder.

Hill streams and stony loch margins are the nesting habitat of this bird and many sites are used regularly. Over 40 pairs were located during a survey of Red-throated Divers in 1983.

The high-pitched 'twee-wee-wee-wee' call as the bird flies off with its 'glide and flutter' flight, is characteristic. On alighting it often wags its hind end up and down like a Wagtail.

Migrant birds are usually seen along the sea shores.

TURNSTONE
(Arenaria interpres)

STATUS: A common migrant and winter visitor.

Small parties of immature birds will be.

seen throughout the summer. Birds in full breeding plumage have been seen in suitable habitat and behaving in an agitated manner, but no nests have been found this century. Saxby gave an account of having found a Turnstone's nest with eggs, though he didn't see the adults.

RED-NECKED PHALAROPE
(Phalaropus lobatus)

FAR: Helsareydi
ICE: Ódinshani
NOR: Svømmesnipe

STATUS: A summer breeding visitor in small numbers.

IDENTIFICATION — L: 6½" (16cm). A small brightly-coloured wader which swims buoyantly and persistently, there is no mistaking this, one of the rarest of all the British breeding waders.

The female has a mainly slate-grey head and upper parts, a white throat and underparts and a bright orange patch on the sides of the neck. The male is less brightly marked.

The bird is usually seen feeding along the water's edge on emergent insect

47

larvae, occasionally spinning in a tight circle to stir up food, and sometimes coming ashore on to a stone to delicately pick off insects there.

The movements seem quick and nervous, but the bird is ridiculously tame, allowing an observer to approach to within a few feet. When it comes ashore to preen it will be seen that the toes are not webbed, but have tiny lobes (flaps) on the sides of each toe to aid swimming.

CALLS — Seems to have a poor repertoire, a short 'chirick' in flight or when it is about to fly off, is the only note heard.

HABITAT AND DISTRIBUTION — This is a bird with an Arctic distribution which has its main British headquarters in Shetland. Even here it is now confined to the north isles although it formerly nested at Spiggie, Levenwick and a few other places on the mainland while Yell, Unst and the island of Hascosay also saw sporadic breeding in the past.

Apart from a few records from Unst, in recent years breeding has been confined to Fetlar where the population is usually in the region of 20 pairs.

Strictly a summer visitor, the first birds to arrive are usually females; occasionally as early as 15th May, it is more usual for birds to appear between the 20th and the end of the month, and this is when the males are usually first reported.

BREEDING — The females, as well as being the brighter coloured, take no part in the nesting duties (apart from laying the eggs).

The nest is well hidden, usually near the edge of a marsh, and incubation is by the male only, the eggs hatching in about 20 days. The male also looks after the young, and as soon as they are on the wing the family leave for unknown winter quarters.

It is unusual to see any phalaropes in the marshes after early August, later records are likely to be of passage birds from farther north.

ARCTIC SKUA
(*Stercorarius parasiticus*)

SHET: Skooty Aalin or Shooi
FAR: Kjógvi
ICE: Kjói
NOR: Tyvjo

STATUS: A summer visitor, widespread in suitable habitat.

IDENTIFICATION — L: 18'' (46cm). Skuas are piratical seabirds related to gulls, with a dashing flight and strong beaks hooked at the tip.

All are dark brown in colour, and some have white underparts. All show a flash of white at the base of the primaries, and have the central tail feathers elongated to a greater or lesser degree. Two species breed in Shetland; the Arctic Skua and the Great Skua, and the Arctic is the smaller of the two.

It is a sleek fast flier, and usually predates terns or Kittiwakes, persistently chasing them until they drop their catch, which it usually retrieves before it hits the sea.

(The word 'skoot' in Shetland means excrement, and people thought the skua was catching the terns droppings, hence the common Shetland name Skooty Aalin.) They come in different colour phases which has nothing to do with the sex of the bird. Dark phase birds are all dark sooty brown, and light phase birds have the underparts, head and neck white with only the top of the head dark brown.

There are also intermediate phases, but all have the two central tail feathers elongated and pointed, with a projection of about three inches beyond the tail.

In the spring and autumn beware of migrating Pomarine and Long-tailed Skuas. The Pomarine is a little larger than the Arctic, usually pale phase, and has the central tail feathers growing into spoon-shaped extensions. Long-tailed Skuas are slimmer, longer winged and have the central tail feathers greatly elongated (up to 8'' (20cm)). They too are almost all pale phase and the mantle is dark grey. Both these Arctic species can occur in Shetland inshore waters, especially in autumn.

CALLS — Arctic Skuas have a loud screaming 'kee-aah, kee-aah' when display chasing.

HABITAT AND DISTRIBUTION — Strictly summer visitors, Arctic Skuas usually arrive in Shetland in the latter half of April.

They can be seen chasing Puffins, terns and Kittiwakes all round the coasts, and are widely distributed as a breeding bird on the heathery moorland, sometimes forming loose colonies.

Many colonies have been decreasing, and in places this is blamed on pressure from their larger relative the Bonxie.

The 1985-87 survey gave a figure of 1900 pairs, over half the total British breeding population. Disperal takes place during August and September and they are pelagic wanderers until the next spring.

BREEDING — Nesting up on the moorland, they lay two olive brown spotted eggs in a scrape in the heather. Of unpredictable behaviour, some will pretend to be injured and squeal about on the ground. Others will attack any intruder, hitting hard and persistently with feet or wings.

GREAT SKUA
(Stercorarius skua)

SHET: Bonxie or Skooi (Unst)
FAR: Skúgvur
ICE: Skúmur
NOR: Storjo

STATUS: Summer breeding visitor. Increases this century.

IDENTIFICATION — L: 23'' (58cm). A large (gull-sized) dark brown, rather stocky bird, with white flashes near the end of the wings (the bases of the primary feathers). The flight is direct and rather heavy. At close quarters the upper parts show a variable amount of tawny streaking, and the neck in particular can look paler in some birds.

The powerful dark beak has a slightly hooked tip and the legs and webbed feet are blackish.

Bonxies are usually seen hunting over the sea and will scavenge around fishing boats, and join other birds feeding on shoaling sandeel. But instead of catching its own food it prefers to attack and rob other birds. Gannets returning with food to the nest are specially targeted, and although they are larger than the Bonxie, they are no match for its ferocious determination. A short chase usually ends with the Gannet being forced down on to the sea (sometimes by grabbing a wingtip or tail) and if the Gannet doesn't immediately vomit up its stomach contents, it is not allowed to become airborne again until it does.

It will also directly predate other seabirds, catching and killing Puffins, Kittiwakes, Shags and others. It is quite capable of killing birds larger than itself, such as the bigger gulls, and it occasionally kills Gannets.

CALLS — Silent away from the breeding grounds where birds will call 'uuk, uuk' as they express displeasure. Mated birds will give a 'wings-up' display, and call a repeated 'agh, agh, agh'.

HABITAT AND DISTRIBUTION — The Great Skua has a limited northern distribution, with Iceland, Faroe and

Shetland holding the bulk of the world population. In Shetland numbers have greatly increased from only a few pairs in the middle of last century to over 5000 in 1985. There is some evidence of levelling out in the last decade.

An ocean wanderer for half the year, birds begin to arrive back in Shetland during the second half of March, and settle into breeding territories on the hills and moors during April. Unst, Fetlar, Yell, Noss and the higher hills of the mainland all hold sizeable colonies, though the greatest density is found on

Foula where the population has been estimated at over 3000 pairs. Census work by wardens gave Hermaness 896 pairs in 1989, and Noss 392 pairs in 1988. There have been a few winter records of birds at sea.

BREEDING — Egg-laying usually begins in the second half of May when two eggs are laid in a scrape ,on the open moors. Parent birds are notoriously fierce in defence of their offspring and will dive-bomb any intruder, sometimes hitting hard with feet or wings. Birds begin to move out to sea from mid-September.

BLACK-HEADED GULL
(*Larus ridibundus*)

SHET: Hoodie Maa or Heedie Craa
FAR: Fransaterna
ICE: Hettumáfur
NOR: Hettemåke

STATUS: Mainly summer visitor. Some winter.

IDENTIFICATION — L: 15'' (38cm). One of the smaller gulls. Easily identified in summer with its chocolate brown head, red bill and legs. In flight the distinctive three-toned wings are pearl grey, with a white leading edge, and narrow black tips

to the primaries.

Some birds show a flush of salmon-pink colour on the breast in spring.

They tend to be gregarious, feeding together (will often follow the plough) and usually nest in groups.

Not so numerous or so obvious in winter, when the brown hood is lost, being replaced by a brown smudge behind the eye.

CALLS — It has a variety of high pitched 'kirr' notes (almost tern-like at times) and is very noisy on breeding grounds.

HABITAT AND DISTRIBUTION — Rather sparsely distributed in Shetland, many move out in winter, returning February/March.

Those staying on in winter tend to be concentrated around the harbours of Lerwick and Scalloway. Few are seen in the north isles after they move south in autumn.

BREEDING — Establishes breeding colonies in marshes, on holms in freshwater lochs and on some offshore islands.

Some breeding places are used for many years and others abandoned after a time.

Nests are made from any vegetable material available and are quite bulky. Three eggs are normal and incubation takes about 23 days. Eggs used to be taken for food but this practice has largely died out.

No comprehensive population figures available but the total breeding population is unlikely to exceed 500 pairs. Most breeding colonies are in double figures.

COMMON GULL
(Larus canus)

SHET: Tina Maa or Picki Maa
FAR: Skatumási
ICE: Stormáfur
NOR: Fiskemåke

Note: The old English name was said to have been Commons Gull.

STATUS: Common resident. Some winter movements.

IDENTIFICATION — L: 16'' (41cm). Like a smaller version of the well-known Herring Gull, the Common Gull is slimmer and more delicate looking. The greenish/yellow beak lacks the red spot on the lower mandible, and the rounder head gives it a more 'gentle' expression.

Although it will frequent harbours it is never so 'pushy' as the Herring Gull when competing for food.

It has a similar white body with grey back and wings, and black wing-tips with white 'mirror' spots.

CALLS — The usual note is a high pitched 'kee-yah' repeated rapidly in display or competition for food. Immatures are best distinguished from young Herring Gulls by having a white tail with a black band at the end.

HABITAT AND DISTRIBUTION — A widespread and familiar bird in Shetland, with many breeding colonies scattered over the islands.

Many move away from Shetland in winter, and many passage migrants may occur in the large autumn and spring gatherings.

After summer rain, hundreds may gather to feed on moths or caterpillars on heather hillsides.

They will join Black-headed Gulls in feeding behind the plough in spring, though they are equally at home along the shores or feeding in inshore waters.

BREEDING — Common Gulls usually nest in small colonies, and these can be on open moorland, among the rocks on the shore or on islets in fresh water lochs.

A fairly substantial nest of dry grasses and any available vegetation is built, and the usual clutch of three brown speckled eggs is laid around mid-May.

Common Gulls are very noisy in defence of their nests and will sometimes dive-bomb intruders.

LESSER BLACK-BACKED GULL
(Larus fuscus)

SHET: Peerie Swaabie or Said Fool. (Saithe Fowl).
FAR: Likka
ICE: Silamáfur
NOR: Sildamåke

STATUS: Summer breeding visitor.

IDENTIFICATION — L: 21'' (51cm). It shares many of the features of its larger relative, but is distinctive with its dark grey (not black) back and wings and the yellow legs. It is also smaller and sleeker looking, about the same size as Herring Gull.

Immature birds are difficult to separate from Herring Gulls, but are generally darker in colour. They also take four years to assume adult plumage.

Watch out for birds of the Scandinavian race *fuscus* which visit Shetland from time to time, they are much darker on the mantle, almost like Great Black-backs.

CALLS — With practice their calls can be separated from those of Herring Gull, especially when in a mixed colony, as they are louder and slightly deeper (though not so 'deep-throated' as Great Black-backed Gull). Immatures are not so distinctive.

HABITAT AND DISTRIBUTION — A summer visitor and an increasingly scarce breeder, spring arrivals are usually recorded in early March, with the bulk of the birds appearing in April. It is more a coastal bird than the Great Black-backed Gull, as its feeding habits are more marine. But it will sometimes join other gulls on a 'moth hunt' among the heather after rain, or be seen following a plough.

It leaves the islands again in September and there are only a few records of winter birds either at sea or in the harbours.

BREEDING — There has been a decrease in the breeding populations this century, though the reasons for this are not clear. They often nest in loose colonies with other gulls. Rocky shorelines or hillsides on offshore islands are favoured, though they will sometimes nest on islets or the edges of freshwater lochs. The eggs, laid in early May, are indistinguishable from those of Herring Gull and fledging follows the same pattern.

HERRING GULL
(Larus argentatus)

SHET: Maa
FAR: Fiskimåsi
ICE: Silfurmåfur
NOR: Gråmåke

Note: In Shetland generally an immature gull is called a Scorie. The species is usually identified e.g. a Swaabie Scorie is a young or immature Great Black-backed Gull. In Lerwick no such distinction is normally made and any gull of any age is called a Scorie.

STATUS: A common resident.

IDENTIFICATION — L: 22'' (56cm). This, the archetypal 'seagull', must be familiar to nearly everyone. It frequents harbours and refuse tips all over Britain.

The adults have a white head and body, with grey wings and back. The ends of the wings are blackish with white 'mirror' spots. The stout yellow bill has a red spot on the lower mandible, and the legs and feet are a pinkish/grey colour.

But watch out for similar size gulls with no black on the wing tips as this could be an Iceland or Glaucous Gull from the far north. Part-albino Herring Gulls can also occur and cause confusion, even among experienced birdwatchers.

Common Gulls are similar in plumage but are considerably smaller (but see under that species).

CALLS — A generally noisy bird, the Herring Gull has a variety of calls. The familiar 'kyow, kyow' and variations which communicate warning or other signals in 'gull-talk'.

HABITAT AND DISTRIBUTION — Widely distributed in coastal areas with concentrations near fishing ports and refuse dumps where there is usually a ready source of food.

Herring Gulls are great opportunists, quick to spot new food sources. With changes in fishing methods and the establishment of new practices such as salmon farming, they were among the first to respond. It is already seen that many birds have become attracted to the voes where salmon rearing cages are situated, where they can take advantage of any spilled salmon food.

BREEDING — Grassy ledges on cliffs, offshore islands, rarely inland but regularly on Lerwick rooftops. Herring Gulls will nest wherever they think they can get away with it.

The usual three eggs are laid in a substantial grassy nest and the young hatch out in about 25-27 days. The young take four years to change from the brown mottled juvenile (scorie) plumage to the fully adult state.

GLAUCOUS GULL
(Larus hyperboreus)

SHET: Burgie
ICE: Hvítmáfur
FAR: Valmási
NOR: Polarmåke

Note: The Dutch name is Burgemeester.

STATUS: Regular winter visitor.

In 1975 one was discovered in a Herring Gull colony on the island of Huney, off Unst. It was mated to a Herring Gull, and the pair raised three young.

The pair bred at the same site for five successive years and although the young were ringed, none have subsequently been reported.

GREAT BLACK-BACKED GULL
(Larus marinus)

SHET: Swaabie or Baagie
FAR/ICE: Svartbakur
NOR: Svartbak

STATUS: Resident and widespread.

IDENTIFICATION — L: 27'' (68cm). There aren't many birds which can be confused with a Swaabie. It is the largest of the gull tribe, with a black back and wings, a white head and body. Adults have a massive yellow beak with a red spot, and flesh-coloured legs. Lesser Black-backs are smaller (Herring Gull size) with a slatey grey back and yellow legs. Great Black-back 'scories' are mottled brown like Herring Gulls and Lesser Black-backs, and are best separated by their greater size and generally paler heads.

They also have the beak all dark in their first year, becoming paler at the base in subsequent years, until they reach maturity in their fourth year.

Black-backs are scavengers and predators, heartily disliked by crofters because of predation on sheep at lambing time.

CALLS — A deep-throated 'ouw, ouw' with variants. Young birds have a high pitched 'plee, plee' food-begging call.

HABITAT AND DISTRIBUTION — Resident and widespread, mainly to be seen around the coastal areas. It will follow fishing boats to feed on discards and offal. You may see them along the shores, where they pick up sea urchins or lumpsuckers at low tide, or waiting patiently

for an otter to finish its meal. They will home in on sandeel shoals, and they will carry off young Eider Ducks. Some birds have developed the habit of living up in the hills where they prey on ailing sheep or weak lambs. Very much the opportunist, it will go wherever food is to be found.

'Storm-roosts' on headlands in winter may hold over a thousand birds, but many of these are migrant visitors.

BREEDING — They tend to nest in colonies. In former times when eggs were regularly collected for food, these were usually on inaccessible sea-stacks and cliff ledges. Many birds now nest inland on the hills, though uninhabited islands and remote coasts are favoured. The large nest is built up of dead grass and other vegetation and is often lined with sheeps wool. The normal clutch is three eggs, which hatch out in about 28 days.

KITTIWAKE
(*Rissa tridactyla*)

SHET: Rippack Maa or Waeg
FAR/ICE: Rita
NOR: Krykkje

STATUS: Summer visitor to the coasts in large numbers. Some winter.

IDENTIFICATION — L: 16'' (40cm). Similar in size and general appearance to a Common Gull, the best distinguishing feature is probably the jet black wing-tips, giving a 'dipped-in-ink' appearance. The primaries are also more silvery than the rest of the back, giving a paler outer wing. The head and beak are very similar to Common Gull, but the legs and feet of the Kittiwake are black wheras

those of the Common Gull are greenish/yellow.

It feeds on small surface-shoaling fish and can often be seen hunting for food well out at sea, when its buoyant, bounding flight with rapid wing-beats can identify the bird (with practice) at a considerable distance.

Young Kittiwakes don't go through the 'brown-speckled' stage like most other gulls. Their plumage is like the adults except that they have a broad dark band across the nape of the neck, and a diagonal black band along the wing, forming a sort of 'flat W'. They also have a black terminal band on the tail.

CALLS — The most obvious call is that which gives the bird its British name; a loud musical 'kitti-wa-a-ak' with variants. Very vocal on the breeding cliffs, it is usually silent at sea, except

when being chased by skuas.

HABITAT AND DISTRIBUTION — Outside the breeding season Kittiwakes are the most marine of all the gulls. They range widely over the northern oceans in search of food, only coming to land in the summer to nest on the high precipitous cliffs. Kittiwakes seldom fly over the land except when they are on migration in foggy weather, or during severe storms at sea when they may come in to seek shelter for a time on the fields. In summer, breeding birds like to bathe in fresh water, and regular flight-lines can be seen from the breeding cliffs to a suitable loch. After their ablutions they then flight to nearby rocks or skerries to preen before flying back out to sea.

They are widely distributed round the Shetland coastline, with very large colonies in places such as Foula, Fair Isle, Noss, Hermaness and smaller ones at many other places offering suitable cliffs.

They start visiting the breeding cliffs from early March, and most are back to a nomadic life by late August.

BREEDING — The nest is made from materials such as wet moss, and in places where small streams fall over the cliffs, parties of Kittiwakes can be seen at their communal moss-gathering. The nest is usually on precipitous ledges and only two eggs are laid. The young stay in the nest until fledged.

GENERAL — Since the early 1980s many Shetland Kittiwake colonies have shown poor breeding success, and a steady depletion of breeding numbers. This has been linked to the lack of available small fish (principally sandeels) in the upper layers of the sea. Commercial overfishing has been blamed for the shortage of fish but there may be other factors involved. Some recovery was apparent in 1991.

SANDWICH TERN
(Sterna sandvicensis)

STATUS: A casual visitor in small numbers.

Two pairs nested in 1955 on an island near Whalsay, increasing to six pairs in 1960. No further breeding attempts have been recorded.

Bigger than Arctic Terns they have a yellow-tipped black bill.

ROSEATE TERN
(Sterna dougallii)

STATUS: Rare vagrant.

The first time this species was seen in Shetland was in Whalsay in 1974, and in 1984 one was discovered nesting in Burra Isle. It was paired to an Artic Tern but not only did that nest fail, all others in the colony did as well.

COMMON TERN
(Sterna hirundo)

SHET: Tirrick
FAR: Fjardarterna
NOR: Makrellterne

STATUS: Summer visitor in modest numbers.

IDENTIFICATION — L: 13-14'' (33-36cm). Only two kinds of terns breed in Shetland regularly, the Common Tern and the Arctic Tern, and the two species are very similar in general appearance.

Both are slim, long-winged and with long tail streamers. They are white and grey with black 'caps' to their heads.

Usually terns are seen hawking for small fish near the coasts, often hovering above the water before plunge diving briefly to catch their prey.

Seen closely the main difference between the two is that the Common Tern has a black tip to its orange-red bill, while the Arctic Tern has the whole of the bill blood-red.

Both have red legs but those of Common Tern are longer though this feature is only of value if both species are seen standing together. Common Terns are paler underneath, and the tail streamers are not normally so long as in Arctic (but beware Arctics with worn plumage in late summer).

Seen in flight they can be told apart with practice. The Common Tern has a slightly less buoyant, more gull-like flight, and its wings seem set farther back on the body, giving the impression of more 'shoulders' out in front.

Watch out for non-breeding immatures, or recently fledged young in late summer. They have a white forehead and dark bill and legs.

CALLS — Both species have a harsh 'kee-aar' and a 'kik-kik-kik' and some claim to hear consistent subtle differences.

HABITAT AND DISTRIBUTION — Terns are strictly summer visitors, arriving in early May. Birds seen in late April are probably passing through to northern breeding grounds.

While Arctic Terns are numerous and widespread as a breeding bird, often nesting in large colonies, Common Terns occur in small numbers only. They tend to hang about piers and jetties more than Arctic Terns do, and are less inclined to join the large flocks feeding on small shoaling fish offshore.

For this reason they may not have been quite as vulnerable as the Arctic Terns, during the recent shortage of sandeels.

BREEDING — More inclined to nesting in small discrete groups, or even singly, among rocks or grass on small islands. Occasionally on the edges of large Arctic Tern colonies. The eggs cannot be reliably told apart, but the Common Tern is more likely to have three.

ARCTIC TERN
(Sterna paradisæa)

SHET: Tirrick
FAR: Terna
ICE: Kría
NOR: Rødnebbterne

STATUS: A common and widespread summer visitor.

IDENTIFICATION — L: 14-15''

(36-39cm). Superficially similar to Common Tern, for the differences to look out for, see under that species. A common bird of the voes and bays of Shetland in summer, they feed on small fish and any other small organisms they find near the sea surface. They plunge dive for their prey but to no great depth, the wings often remaining visible.

CALLS — Noisy, especially at their breeding grounds, their usual alarm call is a screaming 'kee-aar' (the Common Tern often has the first 'syllable' more

extended, 'keeee-ar').

HABITAT AND DISTRIBUTION — Widespread in coastal areas in summer, after arrival in early May. An RSPB survey in 1980 gave a total of 31,794 pairs in Shetland. The arrival of the terns coincides with the appearance inshore of swarms of pelagic fish such as sandeels and young saithe, the main species on which the terns feed their young. If food is scarce in the sea, they will sometimes hunt small trout and sticklebacks in the burns or even hawk moths and flying insects over the fields or marshes.

A volatile species, subject to fluctuations from year to year. Established colonies may be deserted for no apparent reason to set up somewhere else — even on a different island.

Also vulnerable to weather conditions; heavy rain and gales when the young are small can cause widespread casualties. This can have a 'knock-on' effect, as dead young attract predators such as gulls and skuas, which, as well as eating the dead chicks, go on to clean out the remaining colony.

Given an adequate food supply terns can withstand the occasional bad year, but from about 1980 an increasing number of colonies failed, apparently because adults were failing to find enough food to supply the chicks. The situation got worse until between 1984 to 1990 hardly any chicks were reared in Shetland. A dramatic recovery was evident in 1991 when terns had a 'bumper year' with thousands of young fledged.

BREEDING — Nearly always in colonies which can number thousands of birds, two, sometimes three, eggs are laid in a scrape on the ground. Offshore islands are favoured, though some of the largest colonies were on inhabited islands such as Papa Stour, Foula, Fetlar and Skerries.

GENERAL — The failure of the Shetland tern colonies in the 1980s aroused much local comment, especially as the main cause appeared to be the non-appearance of the sandeel shoals. This fish was taken commercially by inshore boats, for use as salmon feed and conversion into fish-meal. This fishery had shown diminishing returns for some years, and in 1990 was stopped in order to conserve stocks. Young saithe also failed to show up in their usual numbers, and this could be as a result of very heavy fishing of adults on their spawning grounds offshore.

The effects of other changes e.g. water temperature, current distributions or pollutants, could also have affected the food sources, but are less easy to assess.

GUILLEMOT
(Uria aalge)

SHET: Loom or Longvie
FAR: Lomvigi
ICE: Langvía
NOR: Lomvi

STATUS: Mainly summer visitor in large numbers. Few in winter.

IDENTIFICATION — L: 16'' (41cm). A medium sized diving seabird, with a 'dark above and white below' plumage and a narrow pointed beak. That is how a Guillemot looks when seen on the sea. Flying to and from their nesting cliffs, they form long lines, sometimes in company with Puffins and Razorbills, and fly with a quick whirring wingbeat fairly close to the surface. They will not normally fly over land (except when lost in fog).

At a distance they are difficult to separate from the similar sized Razorbill, except you are close enough to make out the heavier beak of the Razorbill. In bright light it is sometimes possible to distinguish the Guillemot by the browner appearance of the upperparts. About a quarter of the Shetland birds are the 'bridled' form i.e. having a white outline to the eye joined to a white line running back towards the neck.

In winter plumage the throat, ear-coverts and front of neck are white, and a black line extends back from the eye. On the nesting cliff ledges they usually stand upright like penguins.

CALLS — Seldom heard outside the breeding season when they have a variety of guttural 'arrrr' calls which can produce an amazing 'background' of sound from a colony.

Young birds on the sea have a penetrating far-carrying 'chee-lip, chee-lip' contact call.

HABITAT AND DISTRIBUTION — Although pelagic in habit outside the breeding season, they will begin to visit the breeding ledges in January (and have been recorded as early as late November).

A lot depends on available food but few are seen between August and December. Surveys done between 1985 and 1987 suggest the Shetland population was in the order of 120,000 pairs. Counts from various islands are e.g. Foula: 37,500 (1987) Noss: 37,680 (1986) Hermaness: 16,000 (1989). There are many other colonies such as at Sumburgh Head, Fair Isle, Noness etc.

BREEDING — Guillemots nest on precipitous cliff ledges, sometimes in boulder scree and occasionally on top of isolated sea-stacks. They make no nest but lay the single large egg on the bare rock. The egg is beautifully spotted and streaked on a greenish or blue background and is strongly pointed at one end. This is believed to be an adaptation to prevent the egg rolling in a straight line off the ledge.

Young birds are encouraged to jump off the nesting ledges when only two weeks or so old — long before the flight feathers have developed. They then follow the parent birds out to sea. The breeding ledges will be deserted by August.

RAZORBILL
(Alca torda)

SHET: Sea Craa or Wilkie
FAR/ICE: Álka
NOR: Alke

STATUS: Summer visitor to the sea-cliffs.

IDENTIFICATION — L: 16'' (41cm). About the same size as the Guillemot, but a bit thick-necked and with an obviously different bill. It tends to sit higher in the water, often with its more pointed tail cocked up, and it carries its beak in a 'nose-in-the-air' attitude.

The general colour is similar except that the upperparts are black and not dark brown like the Guillemot. The black beak is flattened laterally and crossed by a white 'chevron' and another white line goes from the top of the mandible to the eye. Both Razorbill and Guillemot have a white edging to the secondaries. In winter plumage the 'face' and front of the neck are white.

CALLS — The usual notes resemble those of the Guillemot and the young also have a loud contact call.

HABITAT AND DISTRIBUTION — Razorbills are in many ways similar in habits to Guillemots. They feed on small fish and fish fry, often in the tidal 'streams' between the islands. The Razorbill is a bit more inclined to venture into the sheltered voes in pursuit of small fish, but nowhere is it so numerous as its cousin the Guillemot.

Relatively few are seen inshore in winter, and birds start to gather near breeding cliffs from late February. A flock of 6,000 plus on the sea below the cliffs of Hermaness on 26th March 1978 gives an indication of the probable breeding numbers. There were 1,500 on Noss in 1981 and census work on Foula gave 6,200 pairs in 1987. Otherwise there is little indication of total Shetland population, though counts at study plots show a decrease in the years up to 1990.

They can be seen well in summer near

the lighthouse at Sumburgh Head, where they nest in fairly open situations.

BREEDING — Does not nest 'shoulder-to-shoulder' like Guillemots, but seeks out more individual niches and crevices. Sometimes under boulders near the base of cliffs.

The young are taken on to the sea at about two weeks old and follow the parents away from land.

BLACK GUILLEMOT
(*Cepphus grylle*)

SHET: Tystie
FAR: Teisti
ICE: Teista
NOR: Teiste

STATUS: Resident and widespread round rocky coasts.

IDENTIFICATION — L: 13½'' (34cm). Known widely by its Norse name of Tystie, this bird should cause few identification problems.

A dumpy little seabird with satiny black plumage, a startling white wing patch and scarlet legs. It has a short pointed tail (which is often cocked up) and a black pointed beak which, when opened, reveals a scarlet interior to match its legs.

This is its breeding plumage, worn between February and September, after which it moults into winter dress which is quite different. Then the head and neck are mainly white and the rest of the body shows varying shades of grey and white.

In all plumages, adults retain the white wing patch. Tysties can be surprisingly difficult to spot on a grey winter sea.

Young Tysties are like the winter adult but are darker, especially round the head, and the white wing patch is mottled with dark brown. Recently fledged birds tend to carry their tail cocked in an even more exaggerated attitude.

CALLS — The only call is a thin reedy whistling 'peeeee' which in flying display chase can be broken into a 'pee-pe-pe-pe'.

This call probably goes beyond the human hearing range. Birds will open their beaks as if calling, but no sound can be heard.

HABITAT AND DISTRIBUTION — Common, and widely distributed round the Shetland coast, the Tystie is resident throughout the year.

A survey carried out between 1982 and 1984 gave the Shetland population as 6-7000 pairs, a third of the British (including Irish) breeding stock.

Most of the Tysties living in the Yell Sound/Sullom Voe area were killed during the 'Esso Bernicia' oil spill in 1979 and it took 10 years for the population to recover to former levels.

Birds tend to gather in moult flocks after the young fledge in August, when they are flightless for a time. Spring gatherings are also a feature when scattered flocks of up to 1,100 have been recorded.

Outside the breeding season it rarely comes to land, roosting in flocks in the voes and sounds. It does however sit on mooring buoys (and sometimes on moored boats). It has recently adopted the floating 'walkways' of the salmon rearing cages for roosting purposes.

BREEDING — Tysties do not form dense breeding colonies, and the favoured habitats are the broken rocky shorelines of the offshore islands, where it lays its two eggs well out of sight in crevices or under boulders. But it may occasionally nest in stone walls, under fish boxes or in the stonework of old jetties. It has even been recorded nesting under a liferaft on the stern of a regularly used ferry boat!

The eggs are finely marked on a pale grey or light blue background. The young are fed on inshore small fish such as rocklings, butterfish, young saithe etc., and stay in the nesting burrow until they are able to fly on to the sea in August.

PUFFIN
(Fratercula arctica)

SHET: Tammy Norie
FAR/ICE: Lundi
NOR: Lunde

STATUS: Summer visitor to coastal areas.

IDENTIFICATION — L: 12" (30cm). With the Puffin emblem appearing on everything from t-shirts to tea towels, a description is probably superfluous, but a frequent reaction from people seeing Puffins for the first time is "they are much smaller than I had expected". They are considerably smaller than Guillemot and Razorbill, and this alone is enough to distinguish them in the mixed flocks which can be seen in summer flying between the feeding areas and the breeding cliffs (the sound between Unst and Yell is a good place to watch this).

Apart from the large gaudy bill and orange legs, the Puffin is clad in the familiar scheme of black above and white below. The only exception being the sides of the head which are pale grey.

Most of the coloured part of the bill is a decorative sheath and is shed in winter time. Young birds in their first winter have a much smaller dark beak.

CALLS — The only calls heard, usually coming from the underground breeding burrows, is a low 'aagh-aagh-agh' in a descending tone.

HABITAT AND DISTRIBUTION — A summer visitor to land, very few Puffins are seen in winter apart from the occasional storm-driven or oiled bird. They begin to appear inshore during the second half of April, at first loafing below the breeding areas. Even during most of May they are unpredictable, sometimes sitting in hundreds along the clifftops, allowing visitors to approach to within a few feet at times. Other days there may not be a Puffin in sight until the evening.

Notoriously difficult to census because of their underground breeding habits, recent attempts suggest the following figures: Hermaness 50,000 pairs, Foula 48,000, Sumburgh 2,500, Clett Stack (Fetlar) 2,500 and Noss 1,700.

There are many colonies of around the 500 mark or smaller such as on Skerries, Gloup Holm, Horse of Burravoe, Ramna Stacks, the Yell Sound islands and others.

BREEDING — Breeds colonially, digging out burrows in grassy cliff slopes, among boulder scree or in the peaty tops of small islands. It lays a single white egg which is incubated for about forty days. The young is fed in the burrow on small fish, mainly sandeels and small *gadoids* as available.

Breeding success has been low at some colonies recently due to the apparent shortage of sandeels.

Most colonies are deserted soon after mid-August.

ROCK DOVE
(Columba livia)

SHET: Wild Doo
FAR: Bládugvá
NOR: Klippedue

STATUS: Resident, mainly round the coasts.

IDENTIFICATION — 13'' (33cm). Formerly the only 'wild pigeon' breeding in Shetland, it has now been joined by Woodpigeon and Collared Dove. The Rock Dove has the familiar 'pigeon' shape and behaviour and is thought to be the ancestral form of all the feral and domesticated birds which are such a familiar sight in many cities. While the wild Rock Dove populations of many parts of Britain have been 'adulterated' by the admixture of 'town-type' birds, Shetland birds have so far been largely free of this. The 'pure' Rock Doves have pale blue/grey backs, crossed by two black wing bars. The rump is pure white and the tail has a dark end. The head and neck are darker grey and there is an iridescent patch on the neck.

CALLS — Not heard often in wild birds, it is the same 'oo-roo-coo' call as in tame pigeons.

HABITAT AND DISTRIBUTION — Resident and widely distributed but nowhere numerous, Rock Doves tend to be shy and to keep to the cliffs and rocky shores. They visit the arable land and parks to feed, and will normally come in to stackyards or the vicinity of houses only during hard weather in winter. Post-breeding and winter flocks of up to several hundred birds may be seen in many places, often on stubble fields, and it seems likely there may be sporadic immigration and passage of birds from overseas, but little conclusive information is available.

BREEDING — Sea-caves and fissures in cliffs are the traditional breeding places, some of which have been in use for generations. Caves such as that on the Holm of Gloup have deposits of droppings several feet thick.

Old stone buildings such as abandoned shepherds 'bothies' on remote islands, may also be used for nesting.

Egg laying is known to take place as early as March and as late as September, but more information is needed.

WOOD PIGEON
(Columba palumbus)

STATUS: Fairly recent colonist to the plantations.

Migrants became attracted to the trees at Kergord in the late 19th Century, but breeding was not recorded until 1939. There is a small population now which is probably resident. Birds also bred at Halligarth in 1973 and 1987 and at Strand in 1976.

COLLARED DOVE
(Streptopelia decaocto)

STATUS: Fairly recent colonist in limited numbers.

First nesting in Britain in 1955, Collared Doves arrived in Shetland in 1964. They bred in Lerwick the following year, and are now firmly established.

Lerwick and Scalloway are the main strongholds, but they may breed in any group of trees as far north as Unst.

After they settled in Lerwick their loud 'coo-cooo-cuk' calls were often attributed to Cuckoo.

63

CUCKOO
(Cuculus canorus)

STATUS: Sporadic migrant which occasionally breeds.

The status of Cuckoo in Shetland is not too clear. Reported calling from various places every year, breeding has been confirmed a number of times, though few eggs have been seen. Young birds still with down on the head which appear in late summer can be assumed to have been locally bred.

SNOWY OWL
(Nyctea scandiaca)

STATUS: One pair bred 1967-75.

Ornithological history was made in June 1967 when a pair of Snowy Owls were discovered nesting on the hill of Stakkaberg in Fetlar. This was the first authenticated breeding of this species in Britain.

Under a 24-hour surveillance, seven eggs were laid from which six young hatched and five fledged.

The area was declared a Statutory Sanctuary by the Secretary of State, and protection of the nest was undertaken by the RSPB.

By agreement with the owner of the land a large area surrounding the nest site was declared a reserve, managed by the RSPB.

The pair of Snowy Owls bred in the same area for nine years, raising a total of 20 young. The main food of the family was rabbits and some wader nestlings.

The male disappeared during the winter of 1975/76. Since then although one or two of the female offspring have remained in the area, no male bird has been encouraged to stay and breed. In 1989 an attempt to introduce a young male, which had been found exhausted on an oil tanker, met with no success.

One or other of the remaining female owls occasionally makes a nest scrape and lays an egg or two.

LONG-EARED OWL
(Asio otus)

STATUS: A casual visitor which has bred a few times.

Long known as a scarce migrant and winter visitor to Shetland, the first breeding record was in 1935 in the plantations at Kergord (Venables).

After several years of increased wintering in the gardens of Scalloway, in 1964 a pair nested among the long heather in the valley nearby. During the next dozen years up to nine birds were to be seen in winter roosts in Scalloway or farther up the Tingwall Valley where an occasional nest was found. After that they faded out and further breeding has not been noted.

SHORT-EARED OWL
(Asio flammeus)

STATUS: An irregular visitor, mainly spring and autumn, occasional in winter. The lack of suitable small mammals in Shetland probably inhibits breeding attempts, although the species nests regularly in Orkney. The only record of breeding was from last century when Saxby claimed he received eggs from Yell and that he found a nest with young in long heather in Northmavine.

SKYLARK
(Alauda arvensis)

SHET: Laverock or Ledyin*
FAR: Lerkur
NOR: Lerke
* O.N. 'ledi' means 'high vantage point'

STATUS: A widespread and common summer visitor.

IDENTIFICATION — L: 7'' (18cm). Easily recognised when it is hovering high in the sky, singing its well-known sustained song, the Skylark is less obvious on the ground when it becomes one of the many 'small streaked-brown birds'. It could be confused with Meadow Pipit (and perhaps with Twite) and there is the possibility of other migrant larks in spring and autumn.

Skylarks are bigger than Meadow Pipit or Twite, have a thicker bill than pipits, but thinner than Twites.

All have roughly similar plumage of light brown with darker streaking, and Meadow Pipits and Skylarks have white outer tail feathers. The best identification feature of Skylark is the pointed crest on the head, but this is only raised if the bird is relaxed.

CALLS — The familiar sustained song is a lovely mixture of loud warbling phrases, usually delivered in flight while hovering high in the air (see Shetland name) but sometimes from, for example, a fence post. The usual flight call is a liquid 'chillip'.

HABITAT AND DISTRIBUTION — A widespread summer visitor to Shetland, the first Skylark song is often reported in the local media as early as February, when birds begin to arrive back from winter quarters. Alas such enthusiasm is often misplaced and flocks may be seen huddled in snow-covered fields in the middle of March.

After breeding, Skylarks again revert to cultivated land and stubble where small flocks may build up, probably augmented by passage migrants. If the weather stays 'open' birds may linger on into winter, but most years it becomes difficult to find Skylarks during December or January.

BREEDING — Not so fond of cultivated land for breeding purposes, the Skylark is more inclined to favour rough grassland, and even the heather hills. The nest is well hidden away in sedges or long grass (rarely among heather) and is a deep cup with usually four brown speckled eggs.

SWALLOW
(Hirundo rustica)

STATUS: A common migrant. A few pairs breed annually.

A common spring and autumn migrant with a few pairs regularly staying on to breed. Nesting was first recorded from Sumburgh by Dunn in 1831. Sumburgh is still the most regularly used breeding area although sporadic breeding can occur anywhere, in outhouses, barns and derelict dwellings.

Usually nest singly but three pairs nested in a storehouse on Skerries in 1952.

HOUSE MARTIN
(*Delichon urbica*)

STATUS: A regular passage migrant which breeds occasionally.

Saxby recorded breeding at Gardie (Bressay) in the last century, and there are a few records from the early part of the present century. Most nests were on houses such as Symbister House in Whalsay, and Quendale House in Dunrossness. A cliff nest at Spiggie Voe was recorded by Evans & Buckley.

One or two bred in Unst 1971 and 1972. Nesting was attempted at Sound 1974, and birds bred successfully at Westerloch in 1975. Successful breeding was recorded in Lerwick 1986, in Unst in 1987, at Quendale and Gott in 1990.

MEADOW PIPIT
(*Anthus pratensis*)

SHET: Hill Sparrow or Teetick
FAR: Títlingur
ICE: Púfutittlingur
NOR: Markpiplerke

STATUS: Summer visitor, widespread and common.

IDENTIFICATION — L: 5¾'' (15cm). Another 'small brown bird' without many obvious features to help the less experienced.

Brown above with darker streaking, paler below with a touch of buffish and with strong dark streaking except on the throat.

When flying away, the white outer tail feathers are often a good feature, but not exclusive because that is also shared by e.g. Skylark, Reed Bunting and others. The beak is thin and pointed, and a good point — though not easy to see in the field — is the exceptionally long claw on the hind toe. Our resident Rock Pipit is a little larger and is always darker, more olive/brown in colour and less likely to be found away from the coast.

Identity problems can be heightened during migration time, because other 'foreign' pipits pass through, sometimes in numbers. Tree Pipits for example, are very similar to Meadow Pipits and can usually only be distinguished by the call.

CALLS — When a lot of pipits are moving through, the ear is probably the best means of picking out any rarities.

Meadow Pipits nearly always call when flushed, a characteristic high-pitched 'tseep' or 'weesp'. The Tree Pipit for example has a more wheezy 'treez' but these things have to be learned by practice.

In the breeding season they have a song; usually delivered during a short song-flight, when it gives a sequence of short tinkling notes as it rises up, then a more musical series followed by a trill as it parachutes back to earth.

HABITAT AND DISTRIBUTION — Mainly a summer visitor, only occasional birds are seen in winter if the weather stays mild.

Returning birds are usually recorded in late March, with song heard during April. Things can be confused during May with birds passing through, and even less clear when post-breeding flocks build up in August and are augmented by more migrants.

BREEDING — As its name suggests the Meadow Pipit is a bird of the meadows and uncultivated parks and hill areas.

The nest is often partly hidden under a tussock and usually contains five eggs which can be quite variable but are usually finely mottled and streaked on a pale background.

ROCK PIPIT
(Anthus petrosus)

SHET: Banks Sparrow
FAR: Grátítlingur
NOR: Skjærpiplerke

STATUS: Resident and widely distributed near the coasts.

IDENTIFICATION — L: 6¼'' (16cm). Slightly larger than the previous species and fairly easy to identify by its uniformly dark olive/brown plumage with less obvious streaking.

The outer tail feathers are smokey grey in typical birds, but watch out for birds which have all the characteristics of Rock Pipits but with pure white outer tail feathers. This could be the Continental race *A.p. spinoletta* which has occured in Shetland. The Scandinavian race *A.p. littoralis* has also been identified.

The Rock Pipit has a rather 'cheeky' behaviour and strong 'tseep' call. It is very much a bird of the rocky coasts, though it will forage round houses and farmyards which are not too far from the shore.

It is quite audacious at times, and will often flit out from the shores to inspect a passing boat. One bird used to attack it's reflection in the wing-mirrors of cars lined up for the car-ferry on Yell.

CALLS — Fairly similar to Meadow Pipit, but stronger. Also has a display 'song' when it flies out (usually from a cliff) and parachutes back singing a repetition of notes which end in a trill.

HABITAT AND DISTRIBUTION — Resident throughout the year, and widely distributed in all coastal areas. Rather solitary for much of the time, about the only time a number will gather might be to feed on flies hatching out on decaying seaweed.

There is some evidence of passage migrants, especially in autumn. The only population figures available are from a few specific areas e.g. there were 26 territories on Noss NNR in 1988, and 50 pairs Skerries in 1973.

BREEDING — Song flight is seen from March, and there are instances of birds carrying food before the end of April.

That is probably exceptional and most birds lay in May. The nest is usually in the cliffs, in a crevice or under a rock.

Four or five darkly mottled eggs are the normal clutch.

67

YELLOW WAGTAIL
(Motacilla flava)

STATUS: A regular migrant which has bred a few times.

Among the several races of Yellow Wagtail to occur in Shetland on migration, probably that most frequently recorded is the Blue-headed Wagtail *M.f. flava*, the race which breeds in Scandinavia.

A pair at Norwick (Unst) with a juvenile in 1984 was the first acceptable breeding record. A pair considered to be Grey-headed *M.f. thunbergii* reared three young near Hillwell in 1987, and two juveniles of un-specified race were seen at Quendale in 1988. A pair of *flava* Wagtails were seen around the Loch of Hillwell in the summer of 1989.

GREY WAGTAIL
(Motacilla cinerea)

STATUS: Uncommon migrant.

A pair bred in Fair Isle in 1989 and another on Hermaness in 1990. These are the only breeding records.

PIED/WHITE WAGTAIL
(Motacilla alba)

STATUS: A common migrant and annual breeder in small numbers.

The more migratory Continental race *M.a. alba* called the White Wagtail (with the grey back) is the one which breeds most often in Shetland. But occasional birds of the British race *M.f. yarrellii* the Pied Wagtail (with the black back), occur on migration and breeding pairs of mixed race have been recorded. Nesting probably takes place every year and recorded sites include quarries, stonework of road bridges, and even in boats moored offshore.

WREN
(Troglodytes troglodytes)

SHET: Jenny Wren or Robbie Cuddie
FAR: Músabródir
ICE: Músarrindill
NOR: Gjerdesmett

STATUS: Resident and widely distributed.

IDENTIFICATION — L: 3¾'' (9.5cm). Our smallest resident breeding bird is so well known that a brief mention of its characteristics should suffice. The combination of minute size, dark rusty brown plumage, and short cocked tail is enough to confirm the species, even if the surprisingly loud vehement song is not heard.

Due to their isolation and sedentary behaviour, some island Wrens have evolved into recognisable races. Shetland birds have been assigned to *T.t. zetlandicus*, darker and slightly larger than mainland counterparts.

CALLS — The commonest note is a hard rattling 'ratchet' call which serves as a warning and contact call.

Song can be heard even during fine winter days, though more regularly from March onwards. It is a series of warbling phrases and repeated notes, delivered in a rather hurried manner and amazingly loud for such a tiny bird. It is usually

performed from a perch such as a prominent rock or post.

There are consistent differences in the songs of different island populations i.e. the Wrens on Fair Isle have noticeably different song phrasing from those on Yell.

HABITAT AND DISTRIBUTION — The Shetland race is resident, but there is evidence of some migration, especially in autumn.

No overall counts are available but Wardens' records show 55 territories in Fetlar (1982), 29 Hermaness (1988) and 24 Noss (1990). Every now and again a hard winter will reduce the population, but they always recover.

Wrens are mainly coastal and occur on most of the offshore islands as well. While they prefer rocky shores, they will also be found along burn banks some way inland, along old stone walls and in kitchen gardens with cover such as bushes. Favourite feeding places include boulder beaches, where they will spend much time out of sight under rocks, or creeping inside rabbit burrows in peaty banks, in search of insects and grubs.

BREEDING — The domed nest is often constructed under overhanging banks along the shores, sometimes in rock fissures or even in ivy on garden walls. As many as 10 eggs may be laid.

The nests are well constructed in sheltered places and may survive the winter when they will be used as roosts.

DUNNOCK
(Prunella modularis)

STATUS: A fairly regular migrant which may occasionally winter.

Has attempted to breed at least once when a clutch was laid at Scalloway in 1965. The eggs failed to hatch.

ROBIN
(Erithacus rubecula)

STATUS: A common migrant and winter visitor.

Occasionally occurring in 'invasion' proportions on migration.

A pair nested at Burrafirth in 1937 and a pair fledged young at Kergord in 1989. Only birds of the Continental race have been identified in Shetland.

69

STONECHAT
(Saxicola torquata)

STATUS: A scarce migrant often occurring in early spring.

Stonechats have bred on a few occasions; single pairs nested on mainland in 1961 and 1962, and a pair were seen feeding young at Dales Voe in 1975. In 1976 pairs bred at Dales Voe, Brae and Cunningsburgh, the latter pair rearing two broods. In 1977 breeding was recorded at Channerwick and Scalloway. Sadly that was the last recorded breeding in Shetland.

WHEATEAR
(Oenanthe oenanthe)

SHET: Stinkle or Steynshakker
FAR: Steinstólpa
ICE: Steindepill
NOR: Steinskvett

STATUS: Migrant and common summer visitor.

IDENTIFICATION — L: 5¾'' (14.5cm). A smart, dapper little bird whose extrovert nature makes it easy to see and identify.

Males have a white rump and base to the tail which they show off frequently as they bob and flirt on fences, rocks or hummocks. They have a pale grey crown, nape and back, blackish wings, end of tail and a 'mask' through the eyes and cheeks.

The underparts are flushed with sandy/buff of varying intensity. The beak and legs are black. Females are browner and less contrasty but share the white rump and tail-base.

In late summer the males moult and become much like the female and at that time the young will be on the wing, looking like a more spotted and 'scaley' version of the female.

Noticeably bigger and more brightly coloured birds seen mainly in spring may be of the race *O.o. leuchorrhoa* on their way to breed in Greenland.

CALLS — The usual call is a hard 'chack, chack' rather like two stones being struck together — hence the local names.

The song is a pleasant warbling and chattering and is delivered on the wing as the bird flutters at no great height.

HABITAT AND DISTRIBUTION — A summer visitor usually arriving early April, occasionally from mid-March. Widespread on broken hill ground, old peat banks, rocky outcrops etc. Not fond of areas of unbroken heather. Often occurs along roadsides, sometimes on rocky shores, but doesn't like to be too close to houses.

No assessment of total Shetland population, but the 700 acre island of Noss usually has between 20 and 25 breeding pairs.

Most breeding birds depart from mid-August, but migrant birds, probably from Scandinavia can be common during September and early October.

BREEDING — Nests in holes in the ground, in piles of rocks, peat stacks etc., where it lays up to six greeny/blue eggs.

Young fledge in June and depart with the adults in autumn.

RING OUZEL
(Turdus torquatas)

STATUS: Fairly scarce migrant.

A bird which is recorded among the other thrush flocks on migration, but in small numbers. It tends to keep to the hills and no doubt many pass through unseen. A pair bred on Ronas Hill between 1970 and 1972, and a pair at Tresta in 1988 and 1989.

BLACKBIRD
(Turdus merula)

SHET: Blackie
FAR: Kvørkveggja
ICE: Svartpröstur
NOR: Svarttrost

STATUS: Migrant and common resident.

IDENTIFICATION — L: 10'' (25.5cm). The male is unmistakable with his jet black plumage and yellow bill. With her dark brown plumage and paler spotted breast, the female might be confused with a thrush, but she always has a darker back. Young are like the female but usually have a more rusty spotted breast.

Partial albinism is not uncommon, and birds with white heads, wing patches and other blotches have been reported. Blackbirds with white patches on the breast have been mistaken for Ring Ouzels.

CALLS — Blackbirds have an irritated 'chook, chook, chook' if they are disturbed, and a 'rattley' alarm call when flying off.

The song is a mellow flutey succession of phrases, individual to each bird, and usually delivered in early morning or evening while perched on a chimney pot or other eminence.

There is also a low warbling sub-song, sometimes heard when a bird is roosting indoors.

HABITAT AND DISTRIBUTION — In Shetland blackbirds are now common and widespread residents, but it was only since the 1870s that they have colonised Shetland. On some of the outer islands such as Skerries, breeding has been recorded only in the last couple of decades. It is said that they did not find favour in Shetland at first, because there was a local folk-fable of a mythical bird which sang on rooftops to foretell a death in the house!

While our breeding Blackbirds are probably resident, those in northern Scandinavia have to move out in winter and, especially in late autumn, can appear in Shetland in huge numbers. The returning movement in spring is never so marked.

BREEDING — Blackbirds have adopted human habitations to a great extent,

71

nesting in garages, sheds and outhouses, and even under the bonnets of cars and tractors. They will also nest in dense bushes in gardens and occasionally in a more natural situation such as under an overhang of an earthy bank, and have been recorded in cliffs. A strange mixture of boldness and touchy nervousness, they will sometimes desert eggs or young if disturbed. They may lay as early as March and up to four successive broods have been recorded.

FIELDFARE
(Turdus pilaris)

STATUS: A very common migrant, especially in autumn when huge numbers may pass through Shetland.

The first breeding record was from Nissetter (near Ollaberry) in 1968 when a pair nested under an overhanging bank of a small burn.

In 1969 pairs bred at Halligarth (Unst) and at Kergord, and in 1970 one or two pairs bred in Kergord woods. Sporadic breeding continued until 1973 when a pair bred on Mousa.

Other records were from Kergord in the early 1980s and of a pair at Voe in 1983 which raised two chicks.

SONG THRUSH
(Turdus philomelos)

STATUS: Passage migrant usually in fairly small numbers, which may breed occasionally.

Earlier in this century the Song Thrush was a more regular breeder, and nested in gardens with trees and bushes on mainland, Yell and Unst. Venables recorded that in 1946 the breeding population in Shetland was in the order of 22 to 24 pairs. Occasional pairs have bred in Lerwick, Scalloway, Kergord and Dunrossness in the last 10 years.

REDWING
(Turdus iliacus)

STATUS: A common migrant from Scandinavia (and Iceland) which breeds occasionally in the tree plantations.

Venables recorded breeding in the Halligarth plantation in 1953 and 1954, and birds still breed there occasionally. A pair bred near Lerwick in 1989.

Migrants on passage in spring are often heard singing.

REED WARBLER
(Acrocephalus scirpaceus)

STATUS: An uncommon migrant through Shetland.

A pair nested successfully at Halligarth in Unst in 1973, the first breeding record for Scotland!

WHITETHROAT
(Sylvia communis)

STATUS: A spring and autumn migrant.

This species appears fairly regularly, though never in large numbers.
A pair bred in Scalloway in 1974, the only recorded breeding in Shetland.

BLACKCAP
(Sylvia atricapilla)

STATUS: A common migrant which has occasionally stayed on into winter.

Attempted breeding was recorded at Scalloway in 1974. A pair reared three young at Kergord in 1987, and a pair bred at Collafirth in 1988.

WILLOW WARBLER
(Phylloscopus trochilus)

STATUS: A common, sometimes numerous, migrant which has bred.

Venables records that Sturrock (1901) saw birds nest building in Dunrossness, and that in 1949 a pair raised young in Foula.
Breeding may have taken place in Kergord woods in 1975.

GOLDCREST
(Regulus regulus)

STATUS: A passage migrant, sometimes in large numbers.

Birds had been recorded wintering in the Kergord plantations as long ago as 1945 (Venables).

Breeding was confirmed in 1976 when a pair were seen feeding young. They may have nested in subsequent years, (and did so in 1989) and there may now be a small resident population in the plantations.

RED-BACKED SHRIKE
(Lanius collurio)

STATUS: A fairly regular passage migrant in small numbers.

Saxby recorded how he watched a Red-Backed Shrike feeding three fledged young near Burrafirth in Unst in June of 1870, and we had to wait over a hundred years for history to repeat itself!

In 1990 a pair raised at least one young in the Dunrossness area of the south mainland.

JACKDAW
(Corvus monedula)

STATUS: Sporadic migrant. A few may be resident for a time.

There are occasional influxes of Jackdaws (presumably from Scandinavia) in autumn or early spring. Venables recorded that regular wintering in the Kergord area had been known since the 1930s and that a few pairs bred from 1943.

The only other area where Jackdaws have been known to breed is in the cliffs at the Noup of Noss and the Westerwick/Culswick area. No recent breeding data.

ROOK
(Corvus frugilegus)

FAR: Felliskráka
NOR: Kornkråke

STATUS: Resident since 1952.

IDENTIFICATION — L: 18'' (46cm). If you see a party of black 'crows' (most of them pale round the beak) in the Weisdale valley area, you are probably looking at some of the rooks which started to nest in the trees when the plantations established in the valley became tall enough to attract them.

Black with a purple gloss and with greyish white bare skin round the 'face' in adults, the only birds they are likely to be confused with are Ravens (Carrion Crows only occur as vagrants in Shetland). Ravens are bigger with much heavier beaks and are unlikely to be seen in the trees or on the fields in parties.

Young Rooks have dark beaks and can look like crows, but a close look will show a more pointed beak, and the feathers on the upper parts of the legs form shaggy 'trousers'.

CALLS — A loud 'kaah' less rough than Hooded Crow, is the usual note. Nesting flocks can be quite noisy.

HABITAT AND DISTRIBUTION — Formerly a scarce passage migrant Rooks became established in 1952. In that year there were nine nests in the 'Lindsay Lee' plantation of conifers at Kergord.

By 1973 the colony had increased to 176 nests, and small colonies became established in other parts of the plantations such as Hoove. 344 were counted in 1979. Further expansion was 'discouraged' and 76 pairs bred in 1980.

It is not known what percentage of the Rooks recorded in other parts of Shetland (particularly in spring) are birds from Kergord. There is probably some immigration.

BREEDING — The nests are built high in conifers in the usual manner of the species. Some sampling of brood sizes has been done; in 1988 the average of 25 nests was 1.8 young.

HOODED CROW
(Corvus corone)

SHET: Craa
FAR: Kráka
NOR: Kråke

STATUS: Common widespread resident.

IDENTIFICATION — L: 18½'' (47cm). The Hooded Crow is considered to be a race of the Carrion Crow and so is designated *C.c. cornix*. Though they are very different in appearance, where the two kinds occur in central Scotland, they do interbreed.

In Shetland the all-black Carrion Crow is only a vagrant and the Hooded Crow resident and common — some would say too common!

It is a distinctive and quite handsome bird, with its glossy black head and neck (with a black bib as well), black wings and tail. The rest of the body i.e. the mantle and underparts, is grey with sometimes a pinkish tinge. The beak and feet are black.

CALLS — The usual note is a raucous 'kraa, kraa' but it has a number of more intimate chuckles and other sounds.

HABITAT AND DISTRIBUTION — Resident and widespread, concentrating wherever a food source is available, such as refuse tips, salmon feeding cages etc. No estimates of numbers are available but loose flocks of several hundred are not uncommon. Several hundred have been seen flying in to roost in Kergord woods in winter.

Clever and resourceful, they can be a menace to other nesting birds, raiding nests and taking nestlings.

BREEDING — Nests are constructed from any available material including bits of wire, sheeps bones, dried tangles (kelp) and bits of driftwood, all lined with sheeps wool. The nest may be on a ledge in low cliffs, on a heather hillside, on a telegraph or power pole or in a tree. They have even nested between the chimney pots of occupied houses.

Up to five eggs, brown marked on a blue background, are laid about the second week of May, and hatch in about 19 days.

75

RAVEN
(Corvus corax)

SHET: Corbie
FAR: Ravnur
ICE: Hrafn
NOR: Ramn

'Corbie' is the Scots name for the Raven, which has been adopted in Shetland. There are place names e.g. 'Ramna Gio' (Raven's Cleft) which suggests the Norse name was formerly used.

STATUS: Resident and widely distributed.

IDENTIFICATION — L: 25'' (63.5cm). The largest of the *corvids* or crow family, the Raven is completely glossy black in colour, including the beak and legs. The large size and the broad 'fingered' wings make the bird fairly easy to identify.

It has a habit of soaring high over hilltops or cliffs, and at times could be confused with a raptor such as buzzard. However, the large beak, and the graduated tail are usually obvious, and the Raven has the habit of 'rolling', flipping over on to its back, closing its wings and dropping vertically for a few feet. This seems to be part of the display and is seen frequently when two or more are flying together.

CALLS — The usual call is a loud raucous 'corp, corp' which in itself often helps to identify the bird. The call varies a lot in pitch and, like the crow, the Raven has other more intimate chuckling calls. It is said that in captivity they can be taught to imitate human speech.

HABITAT AND DISTRIBUTION — Resident and mainly coastal in distribution in the breeding season, Ravens will however tend to concentrate where food sources are available: refuse dumps, abattoirs, sheep feeding places. At such places flocks of over a hundred may gather, especially in winter, but non-breeding flocks are also seen in summer.

Although heartily disliked by most crofters, not much is done about it, and the Raven population is fairly high.

BREEDING — A survey (Ewins 1983) showed 195 breeding territories in Shetland. Of this number fewer than 10 were inland on crags, occasionally in quarries and man-made structures and one in a tree. The rest were on cliffs.

The nest is a large structure of sticks, seaweed, sheep's bones and other material, and is usually lined with sheep's wool. It is often protected by an overhang.

The average clutch is five eggs which are usually laid by the end of March, and incubation takes three weeks.

The young Ravens are fed by the parents until after they leave the nest, and they remain in the vicinity for a while.

Ravens are particularly vulnerable to predation by Fulmars, who will take over completed nests, or spit oil over both adults and young. Any bird badly contaminated by Fulmar oil has little chance of survival.

STARLING
(Sturnus vulgaris)

SHET: Stirlin or Stari (Fetlar)
FAR/ICE: Stari
NOR: Stær

STATUS: Resident and common.

IDENTIFICATION — L: 8½'' (21.5cm). Their plump shape, rather short tail, fairly long pointed bill and generally dark plumage will be familiar to most people.

Gregarious by nature, although they can be quite quarrelsome over food, many city dwellers will be familiar with the huge roost flocks of Starlings which descend on some cities at dusk, fouling buildings and raising the blood-pressures of city councillors.

If Starlings were rare they would be acclaimed for their beauty, because seen closely, the dark plumage is beautifully glossed by greens and purple, especially in the breeding season. At that time also, the bill becomes mainly yellow. In winter there is more spangling of white spots on the plumage, though less in males. Young birds in their first year are mainly chocolate-brown in colour.

CALLS — The alarm note is a harsh 'cheerr', pre-roost parties keep up a continuous twittering. The song, which can be heard at any time, is a rich, rambling series of throaty warbling, chirruping and whistling notes, often interspersed with exact mimicry of local birds. Some will give precise imitations of shepherd's whistles, to the frustration of local sheepdogs!

HABITAT AND DISTRIBUTION — Shetland Starlings have been assigned to a local race *zetlandicus* which cannot reliably be separated in the field, but which have measurably wider bills and are described as being more glossy, and less spotted in the breeding season. Juveniles however are recognisably darker than those of the nominate race and have pale chins.

Widespread and locally common as they are, Starlings in Shetland never get to the stage of being a serious nuisance.

Roost flocks of several hundreds may be seen in many places and the usual night roosts are in sea caves or sheltered places in the cliffs. Tree roosts are of necessity limited but have been recorded.

There is a build-up of what are evidently migrant flocks in spring and autumn — and this is substantiated by records from offshore oil-platforms — and autumn/winter flocks of several thousand have been recorded on occasion.

BREEDING — Starlings nest in a variety of situations; the preferred habitat is probably holes and crevices in stones walls and old buildings. Cliff nesting is fairly common and they will use nest-boxes where available. But almost any suitable place will be used, and nests have been recorded in holes in the ground, letterboxes, and in roof-spaces. The nest is an untidy structure of straw, grass, feathers etc., in which usually five blue eggs are laid from late April. Parties of fledged young are seen from early June.

HOUSE SPARROW
(Passer domesticus)

SHET: Sporrow
FAR: Gráspurvur
ICE: Gráspør
NOR: Gråspurv

STATUS: Resident and common. Some decline due to loss of breeding habitat.

IDENTIFICATION — L: 5¾'' (14.5cm). With nothing much to commend it for beauty, either plumage or song, the Sparrow is nevertheless known to millions. Its cheeky, chirpy nature has probably inspired more verse and prose than even the Nightingale. It is also a 'yardstick' bird when making size comparisons of other species.

The male House Sparrow is actually quite a handsome little bird with his warm streaky brown back, grey crown with bright brown through the eye and over the nape. The pale cheeks and black 'bib' clearly separated from the pale grey underparts is distinctive. The female has similar though paler shades of brown, and lacks the bright brown and grey head markings and black bib.

CALLS — The main call which also forms the basis of the limited 'song' is a fairly loud 'chillip' and a party of birds can get quite noisy.

HABITAT AND DISTRIBUTION — Resident and with a wide, though patchy distribution. Largely commensal with man, Sparrows do not stay long on an island once it has been abandoned.

Formerly much more common, it has retreated with the vanishing crops of oats, and with the replacement of stone walls with fences and breeze blocks.

Sparrows have suffered periodic infections which have decimated whole areas, sometimes for years. There was a very bad outbreak in the 1920s. More recent problems may have been due to the use of seed oats which had been 'dressed' with pesticides.

Flocks of several hundred may still be seen, especially in late summer when crops are ripening.

BREEDING — Nearly always in man-made structures, the favourite situation is a hole in a stone wall. For many years there was a small cliff-nesting colony on Skerries, but this was apparently abandoned in the early 1970s.

Nest building has been recorded in March, and there are odd records even earlier, but late April is more usual, with young birds flying in early June. House Sparrows are often double-brooded and newly fledged young are often seen in August.

TREE SPARROW
(Passer montanus)

STATUS: A sporadic visitor which may stay on to breed.

There have been periodic attempts at colonisation from as far back as 1898.

Between 1900 and 1905 a pair or two bred near Halligarth in Unst, and there were reports of a small colony on Noss which was defunct by 1937. Nesting may have taken place at Burrafirth in 1972 where up to seven birds were seen. Three pairs probably bred at Kergord in 1976, two pairs in 1977, but only one pair there in 1979.

CHAFFINCH
(Fringilla coelebs)

STATUS: A common spring and autumn migrant which occasionally winters.

Saxby records that a pair nested in Halligarth in 1901, and for three years in succession in the 1930s. A pair bred at Kergord in 1973, and probably in 1986 and 1987.

One or more pairs certainly bred in 1988 and 1989, and nesting was attempted (but not confirmed) in 1990.

TWITE
(Carduelis flavirostris)

SHET: Lintie
FAR: Íriskur
NOR: Bergirisk

STATUS: Not clear. Some may be resident, others migrants and winter visitors.

IDENTIFICATION — L: 5¼'' (13cm). Most likely to be confused with Linnet or Redpoll, both of which occur as migrants (occasionally in winter), but Linnets have a plainer red-brown on the upper part of the wings, and males have a rosy flush on the breast. Redpolls have a black chin and a red patch on the forehead. The general colour of Twite is warm tawny brown, fairly heavily streaked, and shading to paler buffish on the underparts. Males have a pinkish rump but this is not always easy to see in the field. The short conical bill is greyish (but yellow in males in winter). The tail is distinctly forked.

CALLS — The usual call is a twangy, almost nasal 'chooweet' and a little musical twitter on taking flight. A party of Twite will often gather on a fence and sing in chorus. The song is a bit like that of Linnet but is more 'twangy' and with fewer 'liquid' notes.

HABITAT AND DISTRIBUTION — Our breeding population is probably resident, but is augmented by passage birds in autumn, some of whom might stay on through a mild winter. Fluctuates in

numbers, but in a good autumn flocks of over two hundred may be recorded in some places, though half that number is more usual.

Wintering parties tend to stay around farms and crofts, feeding on stubble fields and stackyards, but break up in spring when birds disperse to breed.

In the summer they can be quite difficult to find, but a good place to watch out for Linties is along the ruinous wall which follows the cliff edge on Noss, or near the Lerwick cemetery.

BREEDING — Twite like to nest in grassy cliffs, along banks or hillsides and occasionally in gardens. The female always builds the nest, while the male encourages her by flitting around and singing constantly. The five or six eggs are usually laid from late May and incubated by the hen bird. Sometimes they will rear two broods and scarcely fledged young have been recorded in August.

SNOW BUNTING
(Plectrophenax nivalis)

SHET: Snaa Fool
ICE: Snjótittlingur
FAR: Snjófuglur
NOR: Snøspurv

STATUS: Migrant and winter visitor.

Snow Buntings occasionally hang about on the higher hills through the breeding season.

Saxby cited one or two rather unsatisfactory records from Unst last century. A pair was 'anxiety calling' in suitable breeding terrain on Ronas Hill in 1977.

CORN BUNTING
(Emberiza calandra)

SHET: Docken Sporrow. Trussi Lav'rock (Dunrossness).
FAR: Kornspurvur
NOR: Kornsparv

STATUS: Former breeder. Now probably extinct.

When Venables was in Shetland in the 1940s and 1950s, he recorded Corn

Buntings as breeding on nearly all the major islands in Shetland, but that they had become extinct on Foula, Fair Isle and Skerries and Uyea (Unst).

Since then they have gradually declined as a breeding species, with last breeding Fetlar 1964, Whalsay 1972, and Yell 1978.

Singing males were heard in Nesting up to 1979 and in Walls in 1987.

No Corn Buntings have been seen or reported for several years and the species is probably now extinct as a breeding bird in Shetland.

REED BUNTING
(Emberiza schoeniclus)

FAR: Sevspurvur
NOR: Sivspurv

STATUS: Widespread since colonisation in the 1940s.

IDENTIFICATION — L: 6'' (15cm). The male Reed Bunting is a very distinctive bird with his black head and throat and white collar. The white continues up towards the beak in a 'moustache' stripe. The back is dark with rusty-brown edgings to the feathers, and the underparts are whitish with some dark streaks on the flanks. The female is a duller version, the black head being replaced by brown. A pale eye-stripe and moustache contrasts with the dark crown and cheeks, giving the head a distinctive striped appearance.

In winter they may associate with Sparrows and Twite in stackyards, when the white outer tail feathers of the Reed Bunting are fairly obvious, especially in flight.

CALLS — The usual call is a shrill 'tseeep' and a twangy 'tsing'.

Song is usually delivered from a fence or tall vegetation near the edges of wet meadows or marshes, and is an unremarkable series of 'tweet, tweet, teet, tissik, tissik' sounds.

HABITAT AND DISTRIBUTION — Formerly known only as a passage migrant and occasional winter visitor, Reed Buntings were recorded breeding in the marsh between the lochs of Spiggie and Brow in 1949 (Venables). Still confined to that area until the late 1960s it subsequently colonised much of Shetland where suitable habitat was found.

No overall figures are available, but Unst had at least nine territories, and Fetlar four in 1990.

BREEDING — Wet marshy meadows are the preferred breeding habitat, but it will also use reedy bottoms of fields well away from water. The nest is built near or on the ground in a clump of vegetation, and four or five is the normal clutch. Egg-laying takes place from early May, and Reed Buntings may rear two broods.

GENERAL INFORMATION

TRANSPORT

BY AIR — British Airways operate daily scheduled flights to and from Sumburgh Airport, with connections to most major airports in Britain. Enquiries and bookings available from the operators, through local travel agents John Leask & Son, Esplanade, Lerwick, (0595) 3162, or information from Shetland Islands Tourism, Market Cross, Lerwick, (0595) 3434.

Loganair operate daily flights between Edinburgh and Tingwall airport near Lerwick, as well as an inter-island service to most Shetland islands including Fair Isle. Major expansions in services are planned and should be operational in spring 1992 and up-to-date information should be obtained from the operators or Shetland Islands Tourism.

BY SEA — P&O Ferries operate a roll-on, roll-off car-ferry service between Aberdeen and Lerwick. Departing 6 pm most days and arriving 8 am next morning, details of schedules can be obtained from P&O Ferries, Jamieson's Quay, Aberdeen, or from Shetland Islands Tourism.

Within Shetland the main inter-island service is by car-ferry, and connects the Shetland mainland with Yell, Unst, Fetlar, Whalsay, Out Skerries and Bressay (Unst and Fetlar connect via Yell). Mails/passenger services also operate to Fair Isle, Foula and Papa Stour.

Boat trips specially for naturalists are usually available to Noss Nature Reserve, the island of Mousa and to Hascosay and other small islands east of Yell.

The main inter-island car ferries run to schedules which may vary according to seasonal demand. Current timetables for all services are available from Shetland Islands Tourism.

LAND TRANSPORT — There are local bus services of varying frequency operating mainly out of Lerwick to most parts of the Mainland and, via the car ferries to Yell and Unst. While these are generally designed for local needs, they can often suit visitors who have no transport of their own.

Coach tours to various parts of Shetland are also available, and although they may not be specifically designed for birdwatchers they do include many places of archaeological and scenic interest, and many birds can be seen.

Taxis and self-drive vehicles are readily available, and for energetic walkers it is perfectly feasible to stay in one area and explore the surrounding countryside on foot.

While a few people use bicycles, it is not greatly favoured; the combination of hilly country and sometimes strong winds are not ideal for cyclists in spite of the generally good roads.

ACCOMMODATION — A wide range is available; several good hotels cater for visitors to Lerwick, and there are a number of country hotels.

Guest houses can be found on most islands, and more people are offering bed-and-breakfast accommodation than ever before.

Lerwick has a Youth Hostel, and there is private hostel accommodation available on Unst. There is also a wide selection of self-catering cottages and chalets.

Shetland Islands Tourism offer comprehensive accommodation guides with illustrated brochures on all kinds of places to stay.

WHEN TO VISIT SHETLAND — If it is assumed that your main interest lies in the breeding birds, then the season is limited to May, June and July, with June being the peak month. If, on the other hand your interests include bird migration then late April to the end of May and from late August to October could be good, with migrants and breeding birds overlapping. At either end of those periods you should also be able to see something of the arrivals or departures of wintering birds such as Great Northern Divers, Long-tailed Duck etc.

ORGANISATIONS

THE ROYAL SOCIETY FOR THE PROTECTION OF BIRDS has long recognised the importance of Shetland bird populations. Over 50 years ago they appointed voluntary 'Watchers' to look after a number of important areas, and this system operated until 1964 when a full-time officer was appointed, a post I was honoured to hold for over 20 years.

The Society has reserves in Yell, Fetlar, Spiggie and some of the islands in Yell Sound. Summer wardens are employed to look after the reserves in the breeding season, and the interests of the

Society are looked after by a full time Shetland Officer.

THE NATURE CONSERVANCY COUNCIL FOR SCOTLAND have an office in Lerwick, looked after by an Assistant Regional Officer and several staff. They also employ summer wardens to keep an eye on the National Nature Reserves at Hermaness, Noss and Keen of Hamar.

This last is an area of serpentine hillside in Unst with a flora unique in Shetland.

THE SHETLAND BIRD CLUB was founded in 1973 with the aims of promoting and co-ordinating an interest in ornithology and conservation in Shetland. An annual bird report is published, and a newsletter is sent to all members periodically.

Membership is not confined to people living in Shetland; anyone with an interest in Shetland birds is cordially invited to join — in fact there is a special 'overseas membership' rate for those unlucky people who live outwith Shetland!

Details can be had from the Membership Secretary, at 20 Nederdale, Lerwick.

THE SHETLAND OIL TERMINAL ENVIRON-MENTAL ADVISORY GROUP (SOTEAG) is concerned with general environmental problems associated with the oil terminal at Sullom Voe and, under its parent body the Sullom Voe Association, has initiated a comprehensive programme of research and monitoring of the bird populations likely to be affected by the operations of the terminal. This programme is co-ordinated by a full-time ornithologist.

SHETLAND FIELD STUDIES GROUP organise walks all over Shetland and its islands, with a small team of guides who interpret all aspects of the landscape, wildlife, geology and human history.

They also organise many local conservation projects including rare plant protection, wildflower planting on roadside verges and a range of illustrated talks and natural history displays.

Contact them through Shetland Islands Tourism.

RECORDS. Visitors can play an important part in providing additional information about bird movements and distribution in Shetland.

As part of the nationwide bird recording scheme, Shetland has a County Recorder to whom any interesting records or bird counts etc. should be sent. Currently this post is held by Dave Suddaby, 92 Sandveien, Lerwick.

INDEX

STATUS:

W = Widespread
N = Numerous
U = Uncommon (may be widespread)
L = Localised (may be locally common)
R = Rare (a few pairs breed regularly)

S = Sporadic (breeds irregularly)
A = Accidental (has bred at least once)
I = Introduced
E = Extinct (no records last 50 years)
e = extinct (no records last 10 years)

PEREGRINE	*Falco peregrinus*	(R)	36..........
RED GROUSE	*Lagopus lagopus*	(I,L)	37..........
QUAIL	*Coturnix coturnix*	(S)	37..........
PHEASANT	*Phasianus colchicus*	(I,R)	37..........
CORNCRAKE	*Crex crex*	(R)	37..........
MOORHEN	*Gallinula chloropus*	(R,L)	38..........
COOT	*Fulica atra*	(R,L)	38..........
OYSTERCATCHER	*Haematopus ostralegus*	(W,N)	38..........
RINGED PLOVER	*Charadrius hiaticula*	(W)	39..........
GOLDEN PLOVER	*Pluvialis apricarius*	(W)	40..........
LAPWING	*Vanellus vanellus*	(W)	41..........
DUNLIN	*Calidris alpina*	(W,U)	42..........
SNIPE	*Gallinago gallinago*	(W,L)	42..........
WOODCOCK	*Scolopax rusticola*	(A,E)	43..........
BLACK-TAILED GODWIT	*Limosa limosa*	(R,L)	43..........
WHIMBREL	*Numenius phaeopus*	(U,L)	44..........
CURLEW	*Numenius arquata*	(W,N)	45..........
REDSHANK	*Tringa totanus*	(W,L)	46..........
GREENSHANK	*Tringa nebularia*	(S,L)	46..........
COMMON SANDPIPER	*Actitis hypoleucos*	(W,U)	47..........
TURNSTONE	*Arenaria interpres*	(A,E)	47..........
RED-NECKED PHALAROPE	*Phalaropus lobatus*	(R,L)	47..........
ARCTIC SKUA	*Stercorarius parasiticus*	(W,L)	48..........
GREAT SKUA	*Stercorarius skua*	(W,L)	49..........
BLACK-HEADED GULL	*Larus ridibundus*	(W,L)	50..........
COMMON GULL	*Larus canus*	(W)	51..........
LESSER BLACK-BACKED GULL	*Larus fuscus*	(U,L)	52..........
HERRING GULL	*Larus argentatus*	(W,N)	53..........
GLAUCOUS GULL	*Larus hyperboreus*	(A,e)	54..........
GREAT BLACK-BACKED GULL	*Larus marinus*	(W)	54..........
KITTIWAKE	*Rissa tridactyla*	(N,L)	55..........
SANDWICH TERN	*Sterna sandvicensis*	(A,e)	56..........
ROSEATE TERN	*Sterna dougallii*	(A)	57..........
COMMON TERN	*Sterna hirundo*	(W,U)	57..........
ARCTIC TERN	*Sterna paradisœa*	(W,N)	57..........
GUILLEMOT	*Uria aalge*	(N,L)	59..........

RAZORBILL	*Alca torda*	(N,L)	60.........
BLACK GUILLEMOT	*Cepphus grylle*	(W)	61.........
PUFFIN	*Fratercula arctica*	(N,L)	62.........
ROCK DOVE	*Columba livia*	(U,L)	63.........
WOOD PIGEON	*Columba palumbus*	(R,L)	63.........
COLLARED DOVE	*Streptopelia decaocto*	(L,U)	63.........
CUCKOO	*Cuculus canorus*	(R)	64.........
SNOWY OWL	*Nyctea scandiaca*	(A,e)	64.........
LONG-EARED OWL	*Asio otus*	(S,L)	64.........
SHORT-EARED OWL	*Asio flammeus*	(A,E)	65.........
SKYLARK	*Alauda arvensis*	(W,N)	65.........
SWALLOW	*Hirundo rustica*	(R)	65.........
HOUSE MARTIN	*Delichon urbica*	(S)	66.........
MEADOW PIPIT	*Anthus pratensis*	(W)	66.........
ROCK PIPIT	*Anthus petrosus*	(W,L)	67.........
YELLOW WAGTAIL	*Motacilla flava*	(A)	68.........
GREY WAGTAIL	*Motacilla cinerea*	(A)	68.........
PIED/WHITE WAGTAIL	*Motacilla alba*	(R)	68.........
WREN	*Troglodytes troglodytes*	(W)	68.........
DUNNOCK	*Prunella modularis*	(A)	69.........
ROBIN	*Erithacus rubecula*	(A)	69.........
STONECHAT	*Saxicola torquata*	(S)	70.........
WHEATEAR	*Oenanthe oenanthe*	(W)	70.........
RING OUZEL	*Turdus torquatus*	(A)	71.........
BLACKBIRD	*Turdus merula*	(W)	71.........
FIELDFARE	*Turdus pilaris*	(S)	72.........
SONG THRUSH	*Turdus philomelos*	(S)	72.........
REDWING	*Turdus iliacus*	(S)	72.........
REED WARBLER	*Acrocephalus scirpaceus*	(A)	73.........
WHITETHROAT	*Sylvia communis*	(A)	73.........
BLACKCAP	*Sylvia atricapilla*	(A)	73.........
WILLOW WARBLER	*Phylloscopus trochilus*	(A)	73.........
GOLDCREST	*Regulus regulus*	(R,L)	74.........
RED-BACKED SHRIKE	*Lanius collurio*	(A)	74.........
JACKDAW	*Corvus monedula*	(R,L)	74.........
ROOK	*Corvus frugilegus*	(L)	74.........

HOODED CROW	*Corvus corone*	(W,N)	75..........
RAVEN	*Corvus corax*	(W,L)	76.........
STARLING	*Sturnus vulgaris*	(W,N)	77..........
HOUSE SPARROW	*Passer domesticus*	(R,W)	78.........
TREE SPARROW	*Passer montanus*	(S,R)	79..........
CHAFFINCH	*Fringilla coeleb*	(A,L)	79..........
TWITE	*Carduelis flavirostris*	(W,L)	79..........
SNOW BUNTING	*Plectrophenax nivalis*	(A)	80..........
CORN BUNTING	*Emberiza calandra*	(e)	80.........
REED BUNTING	*Emberiza schoeniclus*	(L,U)	81..........